The Problem of the Many

Timothy Donnelly

Wave Books · Seattle and New York

I WILL NOT EAT MY HEART ALONE

Published by Wave Books

www.wavepoetry.com

Copyright © 2019 by Timothy Donnelly

Wave Books titles are distributed to the trade by

Consortium Book Sales and Distribution

Phone: 800-283-3572 / SAN 631-760X

Library of Congress Cataloging-in-Publication Data

Names: Donnelly, Timothy, author.

Title: The problem of the many / Timothy Donnelly.

Description: First edition. I Seattle : Wave Books, [2019]

Identifiers: LCCN 2019011582 I ISBN 9781940696485

(limited edition hardcover) I ISBN 9781940696492 (trade pbk.)

Classification: LCC PS3604.05637 A6 2019 I DDC 811/.6—dc23

LC record available at https://lccn.loc.gov/2019011582

Designed by Crisis

Printed in the United States of America

9 8 7 6 5 4 3 2 1

First Edition

Wave Books 081

for **Lucie Brock-Broido**

(1956–2018)

I will not eat my heart alone

THE PROBLEM OF THE MANY

What Is Real

And though we had fed long and well at the table
    the talk always turned to whether to go on
regardless of what it might say about our moral sense,
    regardless of what it might cost us in the end,
or whether the time had come to surrender,
let the sum of our particles back into the flow
    hoping they might in the longview recombine
        into something of value, or of beauty, but humbler
than the human—not that we'd ever be able
    to judge, not that we'll ever be able to know
        what comes of what we did, or whether it was

worth it, like the towering alien humanoid at the start
    of Ridley Scott's *Prometheus*, how it paces
to the edge of a powerful waterfall somewhere on what
    appears to be a still primarily mineral Earth,
takes one last look at its oblong mothership
surveilling from a mist, removes its monklike robe
    and drinks as if in ceremony from a cup
        of animate metallic ooze that quickly disintegrates
its all too pale flesh, unleashing new organic matter
    into the ecosystem, strands of DNA unzipping
        haphazardly in the rush to mix it up with Earth's

own chemistry and into offspring whose tumble
up it will never witness—not the earliest infinite-
simal blips or suppertime in old Persepolis, not opaque
dawn in Beijing or any single sentient being
separated a moment from the chaos, wholly
unobserved, in whom life sank down as if to test itself,
limitless, dark, spreading, unfathomably deep
and free. As if at play in ether, a meadow of
possibility skittering as axons of foam across the surface
swell of the North Sea. I felt once I belonged to
it in a way I would collapse the instant I began

measuring it in words: waves in blue profusion
dissolving into geological undulations and then
pulses in yellow sand. Here a snake crosses
my path again in Texas, the length of it like a dew-
damp privilege wriggled by a cloud-hid hand
conveying deep troughs and amplitudes back to the sun.
We do go on. Near movie's end, the last known
humanoid of the type to seed life on Earth
is uprooted from cryogenic sleep on a made-up moon
by a crew of corporate human blunderers it then
looks down on with informed disgust, killing off

in minutes all but one. In *America*, Baudrillard
says the products of our imagination remind us
what is real, the way weariness of existence is
how we come to feel, buried in all this abundance,

we are still alive. Hold on tight, my circumstance.
Tonight we're diving in. Tonight we'll find the bassline
   subatomic-style, let particles of us entangle
    knowingly with those of a gold encyclopedia
in the ruins of Vienna or an ear of teosinte across
   an open border, a common source of being, before I
    die—let us be, let being be, continuous, continuous.

1

THE SEA IS PEWTER GRAY WITH GREEN IN IT LIKE MUSIC

The Stars Down to Earth

The sea is pewter gray with green in it like music.
The green is lit in places where the waves begin to rise.

They rise and thin and curve, sieving sunlight through them.
They beat against the rocks until they flatten into froth.

The froth is white like wool. The froth is white like thought
that catches in the hedge or on the barbed-wire fence

strung between the pasture and a narrow gravel road.
The froth is white like wool that stretches into glistening

through the milder rains of March, or in a fog that feeds it
constant countless droplets borrowed from the sea.

The sea is bluer now, with less green in it than earlier.
The sea is architectural but the froth is more like thought

that catches on a thorn and stretches into glistening
after mizzle, after fog, conducting sunlight in the morning

when lambs are in the dew asleep on deep green clover,
when stars fade out of view without a sound but of the earth.

The sea is even bluer, closer to the color I would think
to paint the sea, then something living underneath it,

something rumored of and large, shaken into wakefulness
as clouds arrive like lambs awakened from damp clover.

The hillside is on fire. The smoke is darker than the clouds
and darker than froth. It rises on an angle like a thought

that knits its aerosols into the clouds, almost successfully.
The sea darkens its brow. The sea is blurred brocade

on the sofa in a basement a face is forced into. The lambs
are pinned down by the forelimbs, shackled and hoisted.

The froth is voiceless. What is manipulable is manipulated
almost endlessly. The sea is at its darkest, having eaten

its shadow backwards. It drags the earth it spits out back
into itself like pewter music. Time is on the narrow

gravel road and wool is on the barbed-wire fence as stars
force the wakening into history. The sea is indistinguishable

from sky now, the headlights approaching like a thought
beaten against the mizzle, beaten into droplets hoisted

up like stars from the sea. Something living underneath it
rises from the basement, glistening through the froth as time

feeds itself itself on the hillside, conducting the music
of the sea up to the heavens, and of the stars down to earth.

Stunt

Early on in the undertaking I imagined
    backing out of it. This allowed me to continue

outwardly while inwardly I had stopped.
    Not to make too much of it but everything

followed accordingly. The human in my experience
    will speak until you agree. Agree,

or it will lean too close and bring its hands.
    Protect what refuses by corrupting it

into something scarce. I don't want to ruin it,
    but in reality there's no choice. I agree

about the weather. I agree to the human voice
    in its red declamation. But when what

punishes has penned itself in sleep, I reduce
    what words it uses into a toxin I can sing.

Prometheus

From a breadth of time so nonmonetizable it lies beyond
human perception, from an airspace no nation has ever
laid claim to, emitting intel from the year's first snowflake
intermixed with its last known rose, not yet rankled,
not irrevocably, naked of foot or in expressive hosiery,
pumped-up thirsty or morose for data—I will reenter
Earth's orbit with game plan readied a lifetime in advance,
but open to debate, chance, obliteration and its opposite.

I have been sent here to warn you. The gum splotches
ubiquitous on sidewalks house sufficient genetic whatnot
to repopulate a desert planet. The brussels sprout
is best if boiled, buttered, and salted. The current mania
for roasting it unrecognizable is a construct of hatred.
The Rosicrucians were a boy band. Everyone else
was entourage, cataloguing footage of failures to synthesize.
Love is not love when it insists on comprehending itself.

This is love—and it's spreading outward, as with umbels
of uncertain plants. Science has not yet caught up with
what I'm about to do to that sandwich. Look away:
trust some instinct in the hand to choose your best defense.

I have just now swallowed a tremendous mouthful
of pickled herring. Am I running a bath here, or a brothel?
Whatever I do next, it will be this, or not this: I can't
do otherwise. In this respect, I can be said to be a fatalist

in disguise, bound to textiles I can't predict, incapable
as the goldfinch last to hit the thistle patch, or as implacable.
Vividness is not accuracy. I couldn't be in two places
at once, unless I were a bird. A burning sensation is often
first to notice the salt, to notice wind, to notice a salt
wind rattling at night the house's loose-most casements.
Casualty has its moments. Pandora's box was just a jar
before Erasmus mangled it. A hope kept deep inside, iron-

winged, might well be delusion. I have been sent here
on a mission. What I lack in discipline I will make up for
in stamina. I'm looking into the matter, the mirror, the abyss.
I'm looking into the camera: it's hidden in a rambling
plastic philodendron, escalating my soliloquy up the face
of Mount Olympus. Comeuppance is informal. Music is
from the Greek. The gravity is palpable, the gravity and light
septifurcating endlessly into threads like felt mathematics

or an ordinary sunset shredded by surfactants in a birdbath
made of clay. Hephaestus shaped Pandora out of that.
Athena taught her to weave. Aphrodite gave her grace
and, at Zeus's behest, a bitter longing through the limbs.

We are her children. It must have felt like hoisting up

from the sea's bottom a big blonde octopus, pinning wide

her baffled arms, then staining them an unreal white.

The highest point the podcast said of wisdom is to know

what you don't, which is everything, which was a quote.

I have filled the feeder up but the word still hasn't gotten out.

Persistence of the past depends largely on technology,

including one's offspring and the four-poster bed.

I have come to notice, to understand, and bearing light

snaffled from a star so minor only Alpha Centauri doesn't

take pity on us. I am here to take pity on us. I am here

on a dare, a dime, a lark. The universe tends inexorably

toward disorder. I have come to set fire to and come to set

things right. I am hovering over the flame like a father

assembling a cradle, or as Prometheus did it with it stuck

in a fennel stalk, an aroma of smoldering anise trailing

behind him the whole way down, knowing he could turn

around before anyone noticed, cover his tracks, return

things back where they belonged, and what didn't belong

anywhere could be destroyed, but that's not what he did.

Gifted

My breath sounded more like a recording of breath
than actual breathing, and not a high-quality

studio recording, but something cheap and muffled,
something made on a small, lightweight device

designed to be placed inside a plush white bear
presented to a child on some special occasion—

plush white bear with the sound of my breath in it,
a gift for a child with such low expectations

a toy of this kind should be cherished instantly
and for a long time to come, but no, not this child,

child who isn't quite what we thought, child who takes on
inhuman proportions, who damages surfaces,

who tears the bear apart with both hands and holds
the recording device in victory against the sun.

What comfort is it that the child is ambidextrous?
What he will do with those hands is unspeakable.

All Through the War

I couldn't remember any of it any more than I could feel
the corporate brotherhood at work among my breakfast flakes
or in those protein shakes I drank to keep my strength up.

I couldn't feel the toxicity the way I thought I should:
little silver pinpricks in my liver and then all over my body
steadily proceeding to a brownout in my limbic system,

the not knowing when I was, if or where we were at war with
and for what reason now. All the time I stopped eating
meat again. I stopped eating sugar. I bought four watches,

each watch stopped. I bought a pound of raw rough bulk
lapis lazuli from Afghanistan and I couldn't stop my tongue
from licking a certain piece of it like a dirty blue wedge

of Toblerone to know how it would feel. As for time, I didn't
always feel right with it, especially when alone especially
by the sea, where time widens to include more of itself,

partly because of the motion and partly because of sound,
which is also motion. A decade of drone strikes in the north
couldn't stop Pakistani street vendors from salt-roasting

sweet corn in pans like steep-sided woks. My eyesight grew
worrisome, I felt light tingling in my extremities and left cheek
I imagined meant diabetes, but it turned out to be nothing.

I turned out to be fine. Last week an airstrike in Somalia
targeting an insurrectionist youth group killed a dozen or so.
Yesterday they seized a village in the center of the country.

After my father's surgery, I went to Ireland on my own.
I told the lighthouse keeper I was worried something was
wrong with me because I couldn't stop looking at the water

with all its changing shapes and color. She said we are all
the same here love, all the same. Often in quiet I can still feel
the stone's abrasion on my tongue. I pulled a lichen from

the bronze age megalith with intent to burn it back home.
I made Syrian red pepper and walnut dip flavored with cumin
and pomegranate molasses. There is nothing more delicious

when eating this. How many seeds did Persephone take?
I thought I could cry for my friend no further until I opened
her armoire to lay to rest her scented shirts in an appliance box:

white, off-white, shell pink, true pink, lilac, lavender, blue.
As polar seas warm up, the shrinking difference in air pressure
between the poles and the equator weakens the jet stream

and makes its path wobblier, explaining all this erratic weather
we've been up to. The Senate voted against the resolution
to stop support of the Saudi intervention in Yemen as Trump

took lunch with the Saudi crown prince. I wake with scratches
I can't explain. I order herbal supplements at night online
and forget what for by the time they get here: ashwagandha,

schizandra. I read objects are more like events with longevity.
On average 130 Yemini children died each day last year
of extreme hunger and disease. A Saudi blockade on seaports

stops the ships delivering aid. These are casualties of war.
The instant the technician's needle found a vein, the seascape
on the wall rattled uncontrollably. She whispered the clinic

used to be a funeral home. Trump showed the prince posters
of the assorted planes, tanks, ships and munitions his oily
billions might buy him like an infomercial in the Oval Office.

What use is an adaptogen when I worry my own daughter
should soon prefer the hazards of an underworld to those of this
and social media? I dropped a fossilized trilobite in the toilet

and it cracked in half. Millions of years of structural integrity
finished just like that. Without Persephone it all froze over.
No crops grew. It was almost the end of us but Zeus her father

pulled strings to get her back. This service won't reactivate.
I have come to love catachresis because what's wrong with it is
right: I light my heart with so much emptiness there's room

here in the dark for everything. War-related violence in Libya
left 47 civilians dead this May: 38 men, three women, four boys,
and two little girls to dust returneth. One version of the myth

says Hecate leads Persephone to her mother with torches
at the end of winter. Mother with torches at the end of winter,
some days I just sit back and watch things tear each other

apart. It is winter on and off now through the end of spring.
Emotion is everything and nothing. Same is true for structure.
I said to my daughter on the phone: Be an honest person,

just be an honest person. Be honest, be honest, be honest.
Some days I can't believe what it means to be alive some days.
Some days I think about tearing myself apart but not exactly

with pleasure. Some days I know the strongest feeling is grief
but I believe it must be love: it has to be, has to be, has to.
Some days I feel each cell in my body has its fingers crossed.

The Endless

I saw a yellow butterfly

flying

in my opinion

the wrong way, flying across

the sound

to Connecticut

I saw a cormorant

oily-looking

flying

close to the sea's surface

precisely

as I floated on it on

my back in

the attitude of the crucifixion

minerals in my body

in

conversation with

the minerals of the sea

about the sun

how can I possibly

add

to what's already been said

so well

by the ancients

and said with

an austerity I'll never

know

it is an honor to take

a backseat to the ancients

who knew how

I was a fat white fish

dissolving

under the sold-out stadium sun

like a god

but like a god

I could live through anything.

Apologies from the Ground Up

The staircase hasn't changed much through the centuries
I'd notice it, my own two eyes now breaking down the larger
vertical distance into many smaller distances I'll conquer
almost absently: the riser, the tread, the measure of it long

hammered into the body the way it's always been, even back
in the day when the builders of the tower Nimrod wanted
rising up into the heavens laid the first of the sunbaked bricks
down and rose. Here we are again I say but where exactly

nobody knows, that nowhere in particular humming between
one phoneme and a next, pulse jagged as airless Manhattan-
bound expresses on which I've worried years that my cohort
of passengers' fat inner monologues might manage to lurch

up into audibility at once, a general rupture from the keeping
of thoughts to oneself—statistically improbable I know but
why quarrel with the dread of it. I never counted my own voice
among the chaos, admittedly. I just figured it would happen

not with but against me. A custom punishment for thinking
myself apart from all the others. But not apart from in the sense
above but *away from.* Although to stand in either way will
imply nobility, power, distinction. As for example if you step

back to consider a sixteenth-century depiction of the tower
under construction, you rapidly identify the isolated figure as
that of the king, his convulsive garment the red of an insect
smitten on a calf, the hint of laughter on his face, or humming

just under the plane of his face, indicative of what you have
come to recognize in others as the kind of pleasure, no more
or less so than in yourself, that can only persist through forcing
the world into its service as it dismantles whatever happens

to oppose it, including its own short-lived impulse to adapt
by absorbing what opposes into its fabric. It will refuse to do that.
It will exhaust its fuel or logic or even combust before it lets
itself evolve into some variation on what it used to be instead

of remaining forever what it is until it dies, even when its death
comes painfully and brings humiliation down upon its house.
In the abstract, on and off—as when hurrying past the wrought-
iron fence some pink flowering branches cantilever through

or if pushed too relentlessly into oneself in public—it's hard
not to admire the resolve in that. But there are pictures in which
there is no king. The tower staggers into the cloudcover as if
inevitably, or naturally, as if the medium of earth were merely

manifesting its promise. Often the manner in which it does so
reflects the principles of advanced mathematics, but it's unclear
whether the relationship between the two might be more
appropriately thought of as one of assistance or of guidance.

This distinction is a matter of no small concern to me, actually, because much as I don't want anyone's help, I don't want anyone telling me what to do about ten times more, and if what it all comes down to is that, there's a far better than average chance

I'll just end up devising some potentially disastrous third option on the fly as I wait in line. Elsewhere we find teams of builders at work among the tower's open spaces with no one figure leaping forward as king or even foreman, a phenomenon whose effects

include not only the gratification of our fondness for images of protodemocracy, but also the stimulation of our need to fill whatever we perceive to be an emptiness, which in this instance means electing ourselves into the very position of authority

we had been happy to find vacant. I myself would be happy leaving every position vacant as an antique prairie across which bison once roamed democratically, each denizen of the herd voting for what direction it wanted to take off in with a nudge

of its quarter-ton head, but someone around here has to start taking responsibility, and I don't see any hands going up. So here goes. Sorry. It was me. I built the Tower of Babel. What can I say? It seemed like a good idea at the time. And a fairly obvious take-

off on what we were already doing, architecture-wise. All I did was change the scale. I maintained the workers' enthusiasm with rustic beer and talk of history. Plus the specter of the great flood still freaked the people out every heavy rainfall, so it felt like good civic planning, too—but apparently the whole project violated the so-called natural order of things. I'm still a little shaky with the language in the aftermath, but my gut says that's just some dressed-up way of admitting I was really onto something.

Unlimited Soup and Salad

A little goes a long way when it comes to reality
    and the question of whether we can know it directly

rather than just through the gauze of our experience
    (not that it makes that much of a difference

when you're right in the thick of it, as when performing
    a bank heist, or competitive mummery among

family and friends, in which case your trust that
    the world is as it appears is more or less inviolate

if unself-reflecting, the way a honeybee trusts nectar
    inhabits the petunia, or that her venom sac or

gland or whatever it is will continue pumping its venom
    long after the stinger anchors in the forearm

of the intruder—often merely an innocent passerby—
    having ripped off the hindmost furze of her body

evisceratingly, which is to say along with much of her
    abdomen and digestive tract, plus whatever

else happens to come with, a kind of surrendering
    as means of attack, which reads tragically wrong-

headed in retrospect, although it does lend a vividness
    to the question of to whom the bee's business

end belongs now—the one from whose person it
    juts or her whose torn foreparts lie on the granite

pavement lifelessly from having implanted it there),
    but when appetizers alone can fill you up, why bother

gambling on the main course, it will only distract
    you from what you have come to rely on as fact

relies on its verifiability—in silence and so totally
    you could almost weep for it, the way they do in Italy

at the end of an opera, an era, or even the idea of
    anything familiar dying: a tradition, a truth; an olive

tree fallen to fungus whose narrow leaves made with
    wind a conversation we had found to be rejuvenative

to listen to; whose fruit and oil expressed therefrom
    we couldn't get enough of; whose shade could reform;

and whose earliest ancestor Athena's constant hand
    did unveil in Attica as the greatest gift to humankind.

Diet Mountain Dew

I have built my ship of death
and when a wind kicks up
I'll cut it loose to do its thing
across an unnamed lake of you,
a firefly sent pulsing through
the nonstop estivation of
the verses of our South, who in
its larval phase would feast
on bitter worms and snails, who
emerges from its mud chamber
our planet's most efficient
luminescence, who turns
chemical energy into radiant
energy shedding very little heat,
so will I sail the compass of
you pleased with my cold light.

I have built my ship of death
aglow in sturdy chemicals
and powered up at night like
American Express: I'm all
customer service only minus
the customer, no service to speak

of other than death, you will
know my logo by its absence
and slogan from the past
ad for the sugared style of you
on TV in my youth, it goes
like this: "When my thirst
is at its worst . . ." and then I
let it trail off into the unsayable
or is it just unsaid because
my mouth is full of you again.

A green like no other green
in the dale, indelicate green or
green indecent, surpassing
the fern and sprout and April's
optimistic leaflet some stop
to admire in nature, they take
photographs noncognizant
of other vehicles, you are too
green for pasture, you are
my green oncoming vehicle,
usurper of green, assassin
to the grasshopper and its plan,
I put me in your path which is
the path a planet takes when it
means to destroy another I think
you know I'm okay with that.

A green like no other green
resplending in production since
1940 when brothers Barney
and Ally Hartman cooked it up
in Tennessee qua private
mixer named after moonshine,
its formula then revised by
Bill Bridgforth of the Tri-City
Beverage Corp. in 1958, year
Linwood Burton, chemically
inclined entrepreneur and ship
cleaning–service owner, sold
his formula for a relatively safe
maritime solvent to Procter
& Gamble of Ohio who went on
to market it under the name

of Mr. Clean, whose green
approaches yours then at the
last second swerves into
a joke yellow plays on green
to make blue jealous till it
blows up in its face but I can't
not love the smell of it, citrus
reimagined by an extra-
terrestrial lizard which is to say
inhuman in the way you say

inhuman to me, a compliment
unraveled in the drawl: "Hey
you, over there, you look
so unaccustomed to temporality
I would've sworn you were
inhuman," and time for it after

time I fall, further evidence
of my humanity: I am at heart
no less susceptible to rot
than the felt hat on the head
of the rifle-toting barefoot
hillbilly, your mascot until he
disappeared in 1969. Instinct
says he must have shot his
self in the woods in the mouth
one sunrise when a frost
was at hand and the apples
fell thick and he was way
too awake when he did so not to
think there would be another
waiting like a can of you in
the 12-pack in my refrigerator.

I have built my ship of death
and enough already, every
toxic sip of you preparing for
the journey to bloviation:

I leave to return and return
to depart again the stronger
for a satisfaction being bound
to no port has afforded me.
I have built my ship of death
so that even when I crawl
back down into the hold of it
alive as what unnaturalness
in you can keep me, it's only
to emerge from the other
end of it intact, and perfectly
prepared to be your grasshopper.

Solvitur Ambulando

After the impossibility of the movement
of any object through time was raised in light
   of the fact that, in time's smallest unit,
      no motion can take place (which is to say,
that any given object in it is at rest, or
   if it isn't, then the unit isn't actually
the smallest, because it can still be divided
further, specifically: into a time when the object
   was in one place, and then the time
      just after, when it's in another, and insofar as

any length of time is composed of a finite
number of such smallest units
   during which, by definition, no motion
      can take place, it follows that no motion
can take place in any aggregate of these
   units either—which is to say, the flying arrow
is motionless, a paradox one might
be inclined to dismiss with other oddnesses
   that don't immediately fit our sense
      of what is real, or what it profits us to take

seriously, especially in the face of what

we have to face), the need to commit to a new

    kind of take on what it means to be

        composed, and of how the properties

of the collective won't by necessity reflect those

    of its constituents, paradoxically

arose—the way no atom in my brain tonight

feels on its own capable of wanting to walk out into

    the street to see the stars, but together,

        they still want to, and it feels miraculous.

Fascination

Raleigh filled his cargo hold with sassafras to carry it
    from the New World to England hoping it cured syphilis,

which it didn't, but its fragrance was just heavenly
    enough to make you think a miracle wasn't completely

out of the question. Elizabeth herself looked out across the blue
    hypnosis of Ocean, saw infection in the form of 132

Spanish vessels and prohibited the setting sail of any
    one of England's own, having awakened to a military

need for many hulls; for masts that tower; for wind-
    loud fabrics but bettered with use; for decks seasoned

by the tread of subjects—their finer, British aspects, reserve
    and so forth. Meanwhile, John White, governor of

Roanoke, rich in sassafras but otherwise an inauspicious
    choice for the crown's toehold in the Americas, is

back in town for emergency supplies and aid, but given
    Elizabeth's "stay of shipping," won't be allowed to return

to Roanoke for years. Two long years White pounds his pewter
tankard down, having abandoned wife and daughter

to an end without an author, his tankard cylindrical,
lidded with an acorn thumbpiece, and filled with ale

whose froth spatters on the tabletops in meaningful patterns
he can't yet discern: first the arrowhead of Hatteras,

then a crescent of the Armada, then at last a mitten or
one- or three-lobed leaf of sassafras, frequent thickener

of stews for the Choctaw, who still dry its foliage and grind
it into a powder high in mucilage, which is found

also in quantity in okra, whose seedpods are said to have
been taken from Africa to feed the colonies' growing slave

population as cheaply as possible. High on the list of
heat- and drought-resistant crops, okra means to live

despite untenable conditions and deserves a tribute
unique among those owed to every plant whose leaf, root,

flower, berry, bark or fruit has gotten us as far as this
without complaint: aloe, apple, artichoke and asparagus

to start, then aubergine, a favorite of Alexander the Great
who carried it from India and into Babylon despite

his astronomer's warning that the thunderous local deity
    Marduk had enough already, but the Macedonian was pretty

sure a promise to repair Marduk's temple—in ruins since
    Sennacherib toppled it, and felt by fringe historians

to have been the true Tower of Babel—might serve to soften
    the god's heart. But apparently not. Alexander's coffin,

all gold, filled with rumored honey and carried west, far
    from his deathbed in the palace built by Nebuchadnezzar

centuries earlier, came to rest in Alexandria, founded by
    and named for himself, site where his successor Ptolemy

eventually built the celebrated library that Callimachus
    worked at, and whose fiery destruction was traumatic as

a blunt force to the head of humanity. You can still feel it
    today. Cherokee drank a tea of sassafras root to dispollute

the blood in Raleigh's day, but knew never to drink it more
    than a week at a time. English colonists came, saw

and concocted a copycat tonic that mutated into the diet
    root beer I have here, its frothy head no longer an intricate

play of sassafras mucilage because the FDA determined
    a principle in the root was hepatocarcinogenic to rodent

life in 1960. Now most manufacturers add extract of soapbark
to parrot the effect. In his *Life of Alexander*, Plutarch

recalls that the hero was born on the same day Herostratus
set the Temple of Diana in Ephesus ablaze so that his

name would live forever. Soapbark acts as a foaming agent
in many fire extinguishers. Without his imprisonment

and brace of assistants, Raleigh wouldn't have produced
The History of the World, whose first book states the greatest

wonder of the earth is the palm tree. I have stood beneath
a tall one in L.A. and watched its full fronds seethe

like the mane of a lion. Diana's temple the way the Ephesian
workforce fixed it is remembered as one of the seven

wonders of antiquity, its chalk white blinding under chicory-
blue Turkish skies. I hear the fingertips of history

thrum on tabletops in Roanoke and when popcorn bursts as it
spins in my microwave. When I open the bag opposite

my kitchen window, the night reflects my face back in at
me through the steam expressed from kernels to fascinate

its way back into the water cycle, in order to be the rain
that fed the sassafras we hid in before I had to be human.

Malamute

When I was a dog I pulled the sled with the other dogs
and to the crest of my ability, for never was I a snob about it
moreover never lazy, day into night through the cold
pine forest we were bred to and for which I came to feel
love as fast as others as a blur that slowed around us
at our suppers, then watched us twitch in our heavy sleep.

When I was a dog I pulled the sled with the other dogs
mile on mile convincingly, my tongue construed the forest
no condition not to drape in, identical its pinkness
from my open mouth as theirs, the nylon tapes between us
reinforcing sentiment, a kind relief through constant
focus but from what I failed to grasp, as did our language.

When I was a dog I pulled the sled with the other dogs
who didn't know I didn't know, but that was what we were
meant to be there for to begin with, yet I could follow
them who followed anyone behind us through the forest
where what seemed to know but was a shape without
sufficient contour hovered, and it proved some trouble to me.

When I was a dog I pulled the sled with the other dogs
concealing my disquiet like a shoulder bone the forebears
said to hurry up now bury, but everywhere the dirt

rebuffed my larger purpose, a fortitude from all the earth
had frozen up against me, the paws of whom had brought me
nowhere but to shame to let it drop for another mouth.

When I was a dog I pulled the sled with the other dogs
the way a roof collapses—inevitably, and even as the wind
must always push, or it isn't wind, it's air, and I was air
that had come to think of it, in some trouble to me the others
felt no twitch of, or if they did, our language failed what
must have been its purpose, or I won't soon be a dog again.

The Problem of the Many

1

When Alexander found Diogenes sunbathing in Cranium,
a suburb of Corinth whose many philosophers and statesmen
had clamored alike for Alexander's attention doggedly, Diogenes's
indifference felt special to the king, kind of bewildering,
but in the best way, as with the elevation of a grape popsicle's
color into the most elusive and cerebral gray-violet possible
if you commit to sucking on it full-force—almost as if to surpass
the sun's own aptitude for rendering something something

other than what it started out as. Alexander approached him
therefore with respect, asking if there was anything in particular
the philosopher might require of the king, and in response
Diogenes sighed a sigh that history has no choice but to recall
as philosophical, and, opening at last his eyes to the long
shadow the king cast, said in the company of many the only
thing he wanted at the moment was for the king to quit blocking
his last drops of afternoon sun, which had until quite recently

been blocked by many clouds, themselves composed of many
drops, or droplets, a variant whose suffix serves to diminish
the small thing further, if not in actuality, then at least in one's

perception. However, and don't get used to it, here the two
truly coincide, as the droplets of water that constituted the clouds
over Corinth and surrounding areas, though seldom without
admixture of salt and soot, would not only have looked smaller
to most observers, but in order for them to stay suspended

in that atmosphere, they would have to have been objectively
minute, on par with those released from the drug-delivery device
marketed as the nebulizer, or "maker of mist," familiar to the many
sufferers of asthma, rather than, say, with tears, or with drops
of enzymatic fluid expressed by human hand from the rubbery
anatomy of murex snails in the manufacture of the famed purple
dye named for its origin, the ancient Phoenician seaport of Tyre.
These would run much larger in size. The snail, unfortunately,

held so few of them in the treasury of itself it took as many
as 10,000 (crushed in time and boiled in quantity in vats rather
than each milked individually) to yield one gram of Tyrian purple,
its hue reported to have been first identified by Tyros, a consort
of Melqart, the local god of the sea, commerce, colonization,
and so forth, when her lapdog found a heap of murex on shore,
ate many, then scampered back slobbering all over Tyros's chiton.
Others say Heracles and his own dog discovered it that way

and that's how Rubens painted it: poor Tyros just a nymph now
hovering out of frame, and in place of the murex's trademark
many-spined shell, the dog's unconvincing forepaw rests
on the smooth moon-helmet of a nautilus. Not Rubens at his best.

Either way, Alexander, who felt in his heart his true father was
Zeus-Ammon, not humdrum Philip, making him proud half brother
to Heracles, wanted to visit Melqart's temple on the island-
half of Tyre but the locals didn't want him hanging around any

more than Diogenes did. And so, recommending the lovely
mainland temple instead, they declined, with Alexander riding off
on Bucephalus and in a huff, the sun setting on an era's end
much as it does for us now: the same wide sky deepening
up the horizon in shell-tinted white to white-blue then gradually
closer to sapphire as the sun slips down behind the black of
Earth, the roundness of it apparent through glimpses that waver
like air above lit candles in rooms where forgotten meaning

is restored, and you can almost see it but it's already smearing
out of focus as last clouds achieve a true pink that appears to inch
into watermelon candy in places, as, above, a half-moon tilts
out of time in a field of mature indigo, the chemical compound
of its pigment in many respects identical to that extracted from
murex but lacking the redness that bromine provides, which turns
it more purple than blue. Indigo is the reciprocal, more blue
than purple, and can be harvested fairly cheaply from the cash

crop that bears its name, having been given it when Alexander,
whose army marched as far east as the Asian subcontinent's
northwest corner before giving up and turning back, came home
with black pepper, cardamom, possibly the scalp of an elephant,
and indigo, vast plantations of which would come in time to grow

in Indian soil under British rule in order to feed persistent European

appetite for the tint through the late nineteenth century until

at last a lasting synthetic form of it was engineered in Germany,

whose Wehrmacht marched as far west as the Bay of Biscay,

its waters unloving to seafarers, its airspace in satellite images

a trapezoidal basket-weave of ship trails, or clouds seeded

by aerosols in the crossed exhaust plumes of cargo and pleasure

vessels, but no less clouds for that, no less composed of many

drops, or droplets, none measuring over a few tenths of a micron

in diameter, any one cloud's boundary feathering ambiguously

into the next, but free from all anxiety, and with nothing to prove.

2

Drifting in and out of tearfulness on a bus trip up the peninsula

into the city, a pair of merged clouds appeared to drift like tragedy

apart above the emphatic half-sour pickle green of mid-April

in Ireland. One smaller than the other, they looked to be moving

in opposite directions at different speeds. If it was the smaller

pulled away from the larger over the space of many minutes with

detachment in order to perform its loss as prerequisite to relief

in resignation so strong it approaches bliss, it was also the larger

retreating by contrast into semi-stasis, suggesting stability is only

ever relative. In time, the smaller cloud, inarguably on its own

voyage, and many meters into it, grew more distinct as its outline

grew vaguer with tiny bodies of the same vapor surrounding it
passively by my eye, by turns incorporated into the cloud and then
rebounding off it into cloudlets contemplating an independence
it fell to me to grant them or deny, underscoring again (and again
because I'm human) the difficulty of demarcating with confidence

where it all begins, how many droplets it contains, which merely
exist alongside. If reality didn't need to be defined we might
leave it where it is, but common sense says it does, or something
else inside us, although in practice it has less to do with space
than with time, a desire reaching out from the present into an idea
of the future the subject finds itself in possession of new knowledge
of reality in: something like a handle on it or even like a charm
against it and, historically speaking, a greater likelihood of being

able to yoke it later on, when water needs drawing from the well
or the field needs plowing. Here, it doesn't: the many bright stripes
of young oats pulsate musically against the homogenized chestnut
brown of sun-warmed tillage as a shadow the size of an aircraft
carrier migrates across it. If I draw a border around the classically
soft-sided mass casting this shadow, then I am making a claim
about what is, and is not, reality, which droplets belong to the cloud
legitimately, which are left out. Remembering a cloud is nothing

if not the sum of its constituent droplets, if I draw another equally
arbitrary border around the selfsame mass but this time include in it
with firm resolve or sloppily one droplet more or less than I did
in the previous attempt, I'll be defining a set of particles whose sum

is nonequivalent to that of the first, which is to say, and in a very
real way, I'll behold a whole new cloud. And if I include another
droplet or leave another out, now there's three, now ten, now many,
now an infinity of clouds crowds what still looks like an ordinary

sky with one cloud in it, an absurdity like a sunflower stemming
up from ground so solid you can pull a tractor over it without ever
giving it much thought, or its relative elecampane, said to have sprung
into being when tears shed by Helen in the course of her abduction
commiserated with properties of the land she was torn from,
and what they felt took expression in a flower. All the metamorphoses
of myth make it seem like the human is turning into something
else but in truth it's just the manifold stuff of reality recombining

in response to key events free of regard to what it is humans take
to be necessary distinctions. Extract of its root is indicated for
sufferers of homesickness, bronchitis, or pains of dislocation; also
asthmatics, consumptives, and accidental adherents to bad ideas.
It will benefit breathers of air around manufacturing plants or any air
with too much grief in it. It warms, it stimulates. It permeates
the bronchial tree. It grows in many shady places, eases expression
that has been thwarted. It is a proven counterpoison. It elevates

many not ever at home in their world, home, or status as human.
The plant itself is thought handsome. Pliny said it fastened the teeth.
Some call it horseheal. Others call it elfwort, and say it nullifies
elfin magic. It would be hard to stand beside it and not sympathize.
It would be hard to think of anyone held at its borders or without

consent and sit still. It is ruled by Mercury. The brain is a mechanism
designed to collect, filter, and sort. It is a downy, shrub-like herb
tall as Alexander. From a cache of past experiences it will attempt

to predict the future. Evolution rewards it. Its many flowers pop
like plush gold buttons dozens of flattened bright yellow filaments
nerve out of. Agrippa refers to its medicinal properties as occult
virtues because the intellect alone can never reach or find them out.
It calls for long experience. It will attempt to control the flow
of experience. It will establish relatively fixed points in its extended
networks in light of what patterns it picks up in its information intake.
Some say Helen wasn't abducted. Some say she didn't resist or cry

tears remembered in yellow flowers. Its freshly harvested seeds
smell like frankincense. It often discounts confusion and overlooks
complexity in favor of assurance that life is simple if you let it be.
Some say she stood in a field of them, waiting. It will mirror aspects
of dominant structures and not notice. Some say she had them
in her grip. It is a frequent playground to the honeybee. Many say
she doesn't exist. She is daughter of Zeus, half sister to Alexander.
It can't behold the infinite inside itself. It will only see one cloud.

3

Two floating islands rove like clouds above the surface of the sea.
From the larger grows an olive tree. It is perpetually on fire. Sunset
laminates the water black-tangerine, glistening like the skin

on a many-spotted salamander. At the tree's top branch, an eagle
perches, unperturbed by the flame; at its base, and wound around it,
a fed snake sleeps, cool in the constant wind of the unfolding.
Melqart wants the Phoenicians to rope the islands, to climb ashore.
He has taught them to build ships. He has given them navigation,

perseverance. He wants them to capture the eagle and to sacrifice it.
When the sacrifice is made, the islands will stop floating, fall
into the sea. Here they will build the great city of Tyre, prosperous
metropolis, visited many eons later by Herodotus, who wanted to see
firsthand its temple to Melqart, whom Greek custom smartly
translated to Heracles, meaning its sanctuary harbored none other
than a deified form of Alexander's half brother, making it even more
incensing to be turned away, and brewing up all that next-level

ferocity in him like a battery as he storms Tyre: thick stone walls
fortifying the island, at many points as high as the Colosseum,
having withstood, centuries earlier, Nebuchadnezzar's stranglehold
on the mainland, were long thought impregnable, but now prove
not so, with stones the size of home appliances knocked loose
toppling into the sea, shocking bats and octopi out of hiding places,
sounding as architecture sounds when unwanted blunt force visits it:
the thundering heard widely, and then a painful, less audible part

felt mostly in the bones of Tyrians, many of whom had suspected
all along that Alexander's brassy request to visit the old temple
had more to do with sizing up the island's battlements or performing
a show of clattery dominance than with authentic worshipfulness

in the first place, not that anything could ever get in the way of
Alexander when he wanted what he wanted, and he did, and it was
Egypt, actually, before circling back to Darius in Persia, but strategy
said Tyre, a crucial Persian stronghold ever since Cyrus took it,

had to be secured, or Alexander would always be looking back
over his shoulder anticipating Persian ships. And so with his troops
he filled the half mile between the mainland and the island with
boulders, cast-off broken boats and a mix of beach debris; branches
of local sycamore, dark-leaved, covered in many tiny tasteless figs,
and maritime pine, whose clusters keep dunes from encroaching
on arable soil; and also cartloads of rubble, statuary and irrelevant
furniture from fallen parts of the mainland, on top of which the king

constructed a causeway wide enough for his many war machines
and topped with two siege towers at the end of it, making the attack
on Tyre, city Ezekiel had prophesied would sink into "a place
to spread fishnets," more or less straightforward, albeit with a long
and labor-intensive setup whose material effects are still felt today:
heavy sedimentation has thickened the causeway over time into
a permanent attachment broad as the island itself, and haunted by
all the above, not to mention the 6,000 Tyrian soldiers lost in battle,

30,000 women and children sold into slavery, and 2,000 soldiers
crucified along the shore, asphyxiating in agony for days, invisibly
exchanging air particles with the same Greeks and Macedonians
who pinned them down, who hammered iron through their feet
and palms, who roped them onto crosses, many of the same wood
used for the causeway, and who now lift them up against the sky

Tyros walked under one morning astonished by the unknown purple
leaking from her dog's mouth. From another vantage, everything

on Earth is proceeding normally. Power is shifting; power shifts.
Matter recombines. Already predatory birds are congregating
noisily around the dead and dying like asteroids in the Kuiper belt.
Wild dogs wait to see what falls. Hyenas keep watch sideways
from the dunes, their ugliness to many humans of no consequence
to their success as a species. Microbes always win. To be human
is to be born blind to more than we can see, but also made of it:
Pasts amass like tiny quagga mussels all along our intakes, pumps

and distribution systems unmysteriously, determining the flow of
sense, feeling, thought. To open oneself to more will take more
effort than architecture, or as much, but in reverse: a dismantling
into expanse, definitionless, unexploitable, which is to say as enemy
of the state, just as Diogenes was: a life without property, a life
without loss, no residence but a large clay wine jar near the temple
of the great mother goddess Cybele, burrowed as the hermit crab
named for him burrows, all molecules of him borrowed, but no more

or less with him than Alexander, which isn't enough to exchange
one for the other, although legend says the king, after meeting
the philosopher in Cranium, said if he hadn't been born Alexander,
he would want to be Diogenes, not that we should mistake this for
a measure of humility, or of any enduring principle, as he was young
when he said it, and yet to achieve what many remember him as
great for, because despite displays of largesse and a lifelong love of
the poetry of Homer, Alexander was no Diogenes. He was a monster.

WHO WATCHES OVER THE ENDLESS WORLD ENDLESSLY, OR DID FOR A TIME

ENTRAILS ON THE BLANK OF DAY MUCH AS THE FOUNDER OF A CITY MAKES

ALTAR HE BUILDS FOR THE PURPOSE OF APPEASING THE ALL-SEEING GOD,

TCHES OVER THE ENDLESS WORLD ENDLESSLY, OR DID FOR A TIME: I HAD L

ILS ON THE BLANK OF DAY MUCH AS THE FOUNDER OF A CITY MAKES A SAC

AR HE BUILDS FOR THE PURPOSE OF APPEASING THE ALL-SEEING GOD, GOD

R THE ENDLESS WORLD ENDLESSLY, OR DID FOR A TIME: I HAD LAID OUT M

BLANK OF DAY MUCH AS THE FOUNDER OF A CITY MA S SACRIFICE ON

LDS FOR THE PURPOSE OF APPEASING THE ALL-SEEING G   GOD WHO WATC

LESS WORLD ENDLESSLY, OR DID FOR A TIME: I HAD   UT MY ENTRAIL

DAY MUCH AS THE FOUNDER OF A CITY MAKES A SACRIFICE ON THE ALTAR

PURPOSE OF APPEASING THE ALL-SEEING GOD, GOD WHO WATCHES OVER T

RLD ENDLESSLY, OR DID FOR A TIME: I HAD LAID OUT MY ENTRAILS ON THE

CH AS THE FOUNDER OF A CITY MAKES A SACRIFICE ON THE ALTAR HE BUIL

E OF APPEASING THE ALL-SEEING GOD, GOD WHO WATCHES OVER THE ENDL

SLY, OR DID FOR A TIME: I HAD LAID OUT MY ENTRAILS ON THE BLANK OF

NDER OF A CITY MAKES A SACRIFICE ON THE ALTAR HE BUILDS FOR THE PU

SING THE ALL-SEEING GOD, GOD WHO WATCHES OVER THE ENDLESS WORLD

FOR A TIME: I HAD LAID OUT MY ENTRAILS ON THE BLANK OF DAY MUCH A

A CITY MAKES A SACRIFICE ON THE ALTAR HE BUILDS FOR THE PURPOSE OF

-SEEING GOD, GOD WHO WATCHES OVER THE ENDLESS WORLD ENDLESSLY, O

E: I HAD LAID OUT MY ENTRAILS ON THE BLANK OF DAY MUCH AS THE FOU

KES A SACRIFICE ON THE ALTAR HE BUILDS FOR THE PURPOSE OF APPEASING

, GOD WHO WATCHES OVER THE ENDLESS WORLD ENDLESSLY, OR DID FOR A

D OUT MY ENTRAILS ON THE BLANK OF DAY MUCH AS THE FOUNDER OF A CI

ICE ON THE ALTAR HE BUILDS FOR THE PURPOSE OF APPEASING THE ALL-SE

O WATCHES OVER THE ENDLESS WORLD ENDLESSLY, OR DID FOR A TIME: I H

RAILS ON THE BLANK OF DAY MUCH AS THE FOUNDER OF A CITY MAKES A S

AR HE BUILDS FOR THE PURPOSE OF APPEASING THE ALL-SEEING GOD, GOD

R THE ENDLESS WORLD ENDLESSLY, OR DID FOR A TIME: I HAD LAID OUT M

BLANK OF DAY MUCH AS THE FOUNDER OF A CITY MAKES A SACRIFICE ON

LDS FOR THE PURPOSE OF APPEASING THE ALL-SEEING GOD, GOD WHO WATC

LESS WORLD ENDLESSLY, OR DID FOR A TIME: I HAD LAID OUT MY ENTRAIL

DAY MUCH AS THE FOUNDER OF A CITY MAKES A SACRIFICE ON THE ALTAR

PURPOSE OF APPEASING THE ALL-SEEING GOD, GOD WHO WATCHES OVER T

RLD ENDLESSLY, OR DID FOR A TIME: I HAD LAID OUT MY ENTRAILS ON THE

CH AS THE FOUNDER OF A CITY MAKES A SACRIFICE ON THE ALTAR HE BUIL

E OF APPEASING THE ALL-SEEING GOD, GOD WHO WATCHES OVER THE ENDL

2

Arrows from the Sun

I had laid out my entrails on the blank of day
much as the founder of a city makes a sacrifice
on the altar he builds for the purpose of appeasing
the all-seeing god, god who watches over
the endless world endlessly, or did for a time:

a pile of animals dressed with slender ribbons,
long sheaves of barley or suchlike grain, figures
carved from local wood or bone. It isn't important
what he offers, only that before he can set it
all ablaze, an eagle with wings like oak rowboats

in violence swoops down to grab the choicest
portions of the sacrifice, carries them off in bright
gold talons, releases them in the blue of the distance
and flies away. The founder of the city squints
watching closely, taking note of where they land,

and, setting out to reclaim what the eagle took
in time finds everything is neatly arranged
on another altar, built by the ancients, in an alcove
enclosed by obelisks, their red granite covered
over in marks no one could ever make any sense of.

I had laid out my entrails on the blank of day
to know what would become of me, the way a voice
in sleep now speaks from the altar, the one true
voice of the all-seeing god, god who watches over
everything alive, to say the sacrifice is accepted,

and the city, built on rock, will last as long as time
itself, a citadel of wealth and learning, its many streets
radiating from a central temple, and on its altar
lie my entrails, punctuated in arrows from the sun
as if a crown for the pain it takes to place them there.

Smartwater

Terrors take hold on him as waters. —Job 27:20

Few of days and full of troubles, with all my body
I suspect this beverage, whose cleverness I think
    must be to document where it's been, is, and probably
    where it's going, its tiny sensors made to spelunk
the interior it refreshes, sparkling as they worm
a path through the systems of me—beginning, I guess, with
    the digestive, then via osmosis up from the digestive
    and into the circulatory, on with its reconnaissance till decorum
says we change the subject, which we do, because
    change is the only constant, and I'm just following
        suit: particles, planets, thoughts; but if I ever confuse
my self to pieces, it's only to pull myself back together in time to sing
    on the platform, or as I micturate, the intelligence unit
        in me taking leave: so long, it's been real, don't mention it.

By Night with Torch and Spear

That fire at the mouth of the flare stack rising
    more than three hundred feet above the refinery
contorts as it feeds on the invisible current
    of methane produced by the oil's distillation

process like a monster, the nonstop spasm of it
    lumbering upwards into the dark Newark
night like a sack made of orange parachute fabric
    an awkward number of gorillas get it on in.

I would worship it. The motion, the heat, the unapologetic
    knack of the element to yank the appliance
plug from its outlet, filling the big blue business
    suite of my head with nothing but its own

wordlessness and light. Not now, not knowing
    what I can't unknow, but back on the grasslands
before we ever came to harness it I would bow
    down among the seething life of that primitive

interior and worship the fire taking one bright
    liberty after another. Done listening to fellow
passengers tweaking the fine points. Done rubbing
    the dead end of thinking like a spent torch

against the cave's painted walls to make it burn
　　better. As the train slows down as the track
curves around the body of water the fire reflects in,
　　it is a form of worship. What is it in me that

hasn't yet been killed with reason, habit, through
　　long atrophy or copied so beyond its master
it parses like the last will and testament of a moth-
　　eaten cardigan? It dumps its nice adrenaline

into my system nights I hear the crisp steps of deer
　　on fallen leaves and stop or when looking up
beneath baroque snow or when I lean over the
　　banister along the border of a turquoise waterfall.

All good and well. But the endless hyperactive
　　plumage exploding from this toxic aviary, this sun
of industry descended from the lightning strike,
　　obscures its diabolism with a Vegas brightness

so that what there is to fear in it instead excites
　　me up a biochemical peak from the far side of which
my own voice, grizzled with a wisdom unknown
　　to me in waking life, reminds me of the conjuror

who grew distraught because he sensed the forces
　　he had stirred up with his art would not be
mastered by it. It rattles tomorrow's paperwork
　　where it hangs from the branches of the ancient

timber trees. It messes with my reception, whereas
I do not wish my reception to be messed with.
It tells me to be careful with my worship—that if this,
too, is a resource, then they have ways to tap it.

Cursum Perficio

Humankind is wrong
says Socrates
about the swans
and why they sing
so beautifully
at the end of life.
It isn't because of
fear, he says, but joy:
they can sense
they will soon be
buried in the golden
arms of the god.

Pliny says it isn't
true that swans sing
at death at all,
it's just a myth or
misperception,
although he does
observe with an air
of certitude in
his brief account

that the swan, if
made to starve, will
eat another swan.

For a long time
my cheek imagined
how the ceiling
felt against it:
cold of an otherwise
untouched plaster,
the falling away
of ancient limitation.
We've come now
to our senses, settling
for the proximate
feeling of a wall.

Wasted

One thing I look forward to in an afterlife is
a detailed spreadsheet of all the dollars I've let drop

without notice to the doorstep in disarray as I yank
my house keys out of my pocket in the dark

at workweek's end, bent as I become on nothing
more than doubling down on the bed once I make it

through the door, too numb in the head to know anymore
much of what's happening down where my feet are

other than the planet underneath them still spins—
turning days into years, making worm meal of my body

as I walk with a printout of my life's lost money
into the haze and down to where the water is, sort of

tearful at first to look over times and the sadness doled out
in foolish amounts, which do, as they say, add up, but

it means nothing here, meant nothing all along: I see
life clearly for once, and am just as over it as I ever was.

Shame

It was the sound of your coworker laughter, of the ice
irrepressible in tilted vanilla lattes, of your ease at being
thrown through the world we never chose to inhabit together
fellow passengers whose whatness made me detrain

two full stops prematurely and walk the rest of the way
despite the city heat, a hurt foot, your big proud sun—
I couldn't be in it a minute longer, I needed to disentangle
myself from the sandwich of you: Hamptons tan lines,

long bright teeth, the freakish intimacy of a loudening
failure to regard the separateness you made me reinforce:
nothing on your blotter left unexpressed, a powerfully
ripe cheese, a pounding wave, you pushed me and I went

and will forever as a darkened platform welcomed me—
I told myself what I felt was shame, shame at my inability
to be right with it, to let the people live, to let them take
senseless pleasure saying *I can't believe how much you get*

my special way with animals; is it just me or is it infected;
how do I keep myself from becoming what others want only
to destroy: I said I felt shame, but shame was just the withered
fruit of what I felt, and on the other side of the orchard

swelled relief, restoration, a stronger volume of my own
oxygen at liberty among the trees, a sharpening as of many
pencils in the cup on the desk in my dark office, or of one
in particular—the sharpest, round high fruit on a windblown

branch only I can reach: I twist it off, I polish it, I take a bite
the point of which is the pure cold music I alone can make
and you never hear, like the sound of the pencil as I dull
the point a little, looping it over the paper, taking it all down.

Nebuchadnezzar

We won't get back the hours we mismanaged on all fours
what many years we did the horse, then quivered bull, or drank

chemical lycanthropy: the punishment of a god, his rivalry
by the book, compelling us to chew the grass and otherwise

be beastly in our appearance, but never in one thought
that scratched its point across the vinyls of our meditative

practice in those days, as now, we were always on the scent of
possibility: whether you can love, for example, a human

being in the abstract but still find it difficult to stomach
in the particulars, such as speech, or its behaviors, so often

off in the moral sense, which despite some ardors of the past
and spasmodic form we still keep fucking working on.

That's what makes a king. Thunderclaps are buttercups
from where we're listening, the cobalt blue of glaze on over

twenty thousand bricks an average fleck in Ishtar's eye.
The same is true for time. You can stretch it or compress it

but you can't get it back: the god of it wraps the present
constantly in butcher paper, hands it to custodians who walk

into the walk-in but never out. The dented-up door opens only
in recollections. We found a cave in our exile and we sat

in it like a linnet in its nest, resting for a time that stretched
into an impulse to forage for radish tops, wild carrot, distanter

herbages conquered in a sequence ideal for the absorption
of such nutrients as folic acid, niacin, potassium, and lycopene.

That's what makes a king. Careful diet, frequent cardio,
waterbreaks, putting yourself first and feeling good about it

especially at the workplace, where everyone waits for you
to crap out anyway; knowing when to say no, or no thank you—

now that the sunrise and sunset points have migrated south
we're working on ourself tonight. Wash the sheep's mouth out

with juniper, cut into its side and slide the jiggly liver loose
and onto a platter to read: all the divots and the swollen spots

not the outline of the city as it is, but as it might be, double-
ringed in walls twenty-five feet thick to protect our coworkers'

particulars as they fall away as they power down as they sleep
in interchangeable but smartly furnished domiciles of clay.

That's what a king makes. Don't tell your dreams to anyone
who won't take your meat. They'll worm them into curses

genetically perfected to attack you in the throne room softly
at first, then graduating up into the big booming voice that spoke

down to us from a cloud at a point when Rome was just
disorganized mud huts. We built canals. We built the above-

mentioned walls and covered them in bulls, lions, dragons.
Traditionally it's thought we built the famous hanging gardens

but some recent archaeological trends suggest we didn't.
Let's just say we did. Let's just say a hidden god who wants

endlessly to be praised has no place telling us to be modest.
Look at all the lollipops that jangle from the rooftops as if

the bold fruits of our own synthesis. Let's spoil our royal supper.
Let's spoil our supper twice and eat when we the king say eat.

A Habitation of Jackals, a Court for Ostriches

Very dark now I put a seed in my mouth but its texture and taste
are too unfamiliar! I spit this strange seed out. I do this over
and over, forty-five times before understanding I must
no longer think of myself as the same seed-eating creature

I have erstwhile known myself to be. The seeds of this enclave
have turned overnight, or else worsened so gradually
I only see it now—now and with disgust because they've
really overdone it. Taken it too far. I mean, it's just silly.

These seeds are not the seeds my ancestors fought for!
Fought hard for. Very hard for. Bitterly hard for even after death.
They taste bitter. There's a bitterness. And they're softer
than a seed should be—too soft. I'd rather eat stones instead.

Stones that my ancestors would recognize as stones!
Stones that my ancestors walked on with dignity. Real dignity.
May very well have walked on. I can say with confidence
that this probably happened. Back when this was a great city,

things happened. That's how it was. Now I'm no longer
that seed-eating creature. Now I eat stones. I eat the stones
of this zip code, and behold—they're already making me stronger.
I am almost too strong. So strong I'm about to announce

the birth of a child. There it goes! A great stone-eating child just leapt from my mouth. There's more where that came from, believe me. Not a problem. But that one came first and as first it shall rule by my side. Till the sun bursts in on our kingdom.

Chemical Life

Often I'll think back to the twenty-five caged fish
    softly lowered into Snow Creek to assess the toxicity
of the waters that the unspeakable chemical company
    released its wastes into over decades and how
        all of them, all twenty-five, lost their equilibrium

more or less immediately, how three minutes later
    blood billowed from their gills like naturalized fuchsia
loosened from a hedgerow four thousand miles away
    and how, shortly after that, every one of them had finished
        early with this life, as did the people of Alabama

who fished and swam and drank from the great
    Choccolocco Creek the smaller Snow Creek fed
its bad chemistry into, on and on without any advisory
    from the many who knew, the long processions
        shuddering in time from church to gravesite silently

as cellophane across the lethal waters. So much life
    destroyed by the elements thought to have given rise
to it in the first place as the energy and phosphorus
    carried here on the backs of meteorites that landed
        in pools of acids frothing at the bases of volcanoes

made available key enzymes required for what science
now calls chemical life, meaning the intermediary step
between inorganic rock and the earth's first ever
spontaneously formed and truly living cell, which I
liken to a widened, ambitious, and unblinking eyeball.

First living cell, what have you to say for yourself
now? I see the dumbstruck circle of you spinning late
at night tonight on my monitor billions of years before
language and I head down to the nearby 24-hour bodega
for a cyan Powerade and I'm practically plowed over

by an ardent garbage truck, one in whose overcrowded
bin your double might be brewing even as it narrowly
whizzes me by—another stab at life, this time hewn
from the fudges, drizzles and perfumes of an unstoppable
crapulence. But here's the thing: there was only

one chance for you to happen hereabouts and after
that, any new-formed organism rolling out of the murk
would fall prey to all the preexisting organisms
soon as it lurched into being. So you're pretty much
a miracle, first living cell. But still my heart is heavy.

Don't look at me, I can feel you say, it isn't mere life
that's the problem here so much as something neither
I nor my offspring ever predicted. We had big doings
planned for the planet till some random event knocked it in
a direction we never wanted and still can't fathom.

We're into birdsong as much as anyone, not so much

    all this willful endangerment. But look at you there, up

all night on the trail of a void. Wade into the world

    a little less deeply. Lie down in the shallows and let it stick

        its infinite leech mouths to whatever ails you, because

as much as you want to fix what is, what is wants to fix

    you more. Unload on it your carbon, your phosphorus.

Your bones' calcium will be good for plant life, ditto

    all that potassium. Not to mention your hydrogen, if it ever

        escapes our atmosphere, might one day power a star.

The Radiance of a Thousand Suns

When on the orange chair to the left of my daughter I sat
with a laptop to watch for a third time the video
comparing Earth's dimensions to those of other planets

and upward to the stars, starting out of courtesy
or something like it with the moon, then followed by
Mercury, moonlike, only slightly larger, and dented over

comparably with craters from having been struck
all its life without atmosphere by asteroids and comets,
then Mars with its redness, no more than a topcoat

of fine ferric dust, then off to Venus, Earth's sparkling
toxic twin, I said there's no getting used to this,
meaning the leap next to Neptune, Saturn, Jupiter,

horrid symphonic music escalating as our sun scrolls
proudly into view, more than 100 times the width of Earth,
but now Sirius, now Pollux, now Arcturus and Antares,

the sun dropping from memory like a penny to the floor
of a carousel in Singapore, now Betelgeuse perched
on the right shoulder of Orion: a falcon into which

two quadrillion Earths could fit, and then at last a star

against whose vastness Earth is no more than a pinprick

to the skin of the orange split like an atom between us

at home with a terror we inhabit in absentia, like a hurricane

on purpose, an enormity we absorb without knowing

it firsthand but from a 4-min video we click to play again.

All the Shrimp I Can Eat

They are swimming away from me at the speed of light
They are telling me this is their preferred way to die

The conversion en masse into a single stream of brightness
Not the tenebrous slog through my digestive process

I say that's only one part of a complex corporate sacrifice
They say fair enough but it's the part we'd like to emphasize

Then take off, all you shrimp, you only call to mind how often
To live has felt like the long, drawn-out migration

Through the body of a god, one who elects to eat each of us
If not out of hunger, then boredom, or in an act of love impervious

To human reasoning (very possibly it's all three at once)
And our birth is when he swallows, and his acids are events

That break us down, and after he's extracted from
Our bodily existence what he needs, the gritty residuum

At bottom is what we call the soul, and this he then exerts
Through his infinite wisdom, grinds into a powder, and snorts.

Golden

Everything will be fine, to paraphrase the anchoress, and everything
  will be golden, like a crock
of manuka honey or handpicked Bartlett pear, or like the calf
  Aaron made out of earrings for the Israelites

who wanted a little something to sink their worship into, having
  already waited long enough already
for Moses to return from the top of Mount Sinai. There he carried on
  with the godhead in the form of a nonstop

burning bush Rastafarians equate with cannabis, which probably
  would have come in handy as the Lord's
nerves frayed overhead like gray cotton candy, having freed His people
  from bondage only to watch as they broke at least one

if not three of His commandments—which, to be fair, hadn't yet been
  presented to them as such, so
there's that . . . Regardless, Moses had to scramble to talk
  Yahweh down from wanting to slaughter each and every calf-

lover among them and just start over, saying what would posterity
  think of Him to hear
He had delivered the chosen out of bondage only to kill them in the desert
  over a little craft project, although with no one left standing

to speak of, God's motives would likely go unknown. Knowability
     is felt by many to lie
at the heart of the imbroglio, as humans like to worship
     mostly what they can know, or at least feast eyes on, and without

Moses, the Israelites lost focus, or lacked insight, or else just got
     swept up. In the end, He Who Is
recalculated, deciding he could make his point with a sacrifice
     of a mere 3,000, or the year-round population of Wellfleet, Mass.,

birthplace of America's transatlantic wireless, and off whose banky shore
     Capt. Sam Bellamy, pirate, went down with
the *Whydah*, a slave ship until he captured it in 1717, its hold
     said to be carrying five tons of indigo, silver, gold dust, and gold.

Lunch in a Town Named After a Company Slowly Poisoning Its Residents

I saw a cow once on a hilltop casually stretch her neck
to face behind herself so that her hind leg might scratch

between her eyes with her hoof. I can't emphasize enough
how casually she pulled this off, while obviously I was

gobsmacked, having never seen a cow do that before
and having never given thought to whether it was possible.

Well, it's possible. Things slid back to normal after that
despite life's electric charge, which I don't let get the better of me.

Sometimes I feel like something might be underway,
but I just wait it out: hands on the table, eyes on the wall.

Meanwhile, it's safe to say the cow is long since gone.
Not on account of what I saw, but because I saw it long ago.

A cow's life expectancy is only fifteen years or so.
Me, I'm right here: red beans on yellow rice, a slightly

brown avocado. The day started off in clouds and the clouds
don't always part. To ask too much of life would spoil it.

After Callimachus

*These Telchines are called by some writers charmers and enchanters, who
besprinkle animals and plants, with a view to destroy them, with the water of
the Styx, mingled with sulphur. Others on the contrary say, that they were
persons who excelled in certain mechanical arts. . . .*

    —*Geographica*, Strabo

Tartarus's footless offspring who spray fans of glyphosate
    mixed with Styx water over farmland regularly,
technicians of *os agrotóxicos* for cash, I am weaponless
    against you, plus preoccupied by a to-do list longer than

an epic—what you've done to my popcorn, my popcorn
    does to me, bowl after bowl of it as I take the documentary
about you in in fits between dark washes and a trip
    to the True Value for drywall mud to repair the divot
        the doorknob to the bathroom door put in the drywall.

Be that as it may, I will think ill of you
    with every other step
        and curse the way you worm
even into the baguette, which in Paris you can buy
    from vendors on the Pont Neuf

ridiculous with butter and the ham on it
    sliced thin, but piled up thick—
        I'm halfway there, I hesitate, I click

on the petition aimed against you as I reach
    out inwardly for France's
national sandwich, with somewhere
        over a billion managed every year although
    it keeps losing ground
to the hamburger annually. Maybe when you're done
        devising ways to make me sick, neurodegenerative
        disorders and the like, but before
        Zeus's thunderbolts lock in, you can

shed some light on that, if not the following:
    at what point do you suspect a versified address
to you begins to take the place
        of legitimate action? Stevens says poetry
    is escapism in "a non-pejorative sense," a break from the
swelter of the real such that when we return to it
        we'll be the better equipped to suffer its ongoing

indignity, poke back a little, tinker with the motor
    till it doesn't rattle so displeasingly on the long drive out
        to the "open countryside"
Nietzsche says we enjoy so much because it pays us
    no attention, by which I think he means
    it has no designs on us, i.e., since the landscape lacks

what we identify as sense, we don't feel ourselves
        falling under the spell of its perception—
we aren't objectified by it, but instead exist within it purely
        as perceiving subject.

        Here the wolf god Apollo
        says don't take his word for it, go outside
and see for yourself

        how the landscape relates
or doesn't relate to you.

        Let what happens in the poem
be what the poem
        makes happen, or at least

what wouldn't have happened if the poem

        had not been.
                Let it then

        be a record not only
        of its own becoming, but of another
change it brought about.
                        In this way it might be felt

        the poem isn't as much an escape
                from reality, but a portal back into it.

One night I will walk out under a sky so clear
    I'll forget you are everywhere. The stars will baffle me

with numbers as they arc
    in all directions down
to the horizon as they must have when Callimachus
    wrote that he preferred
        the "delicate wings" of the cicada
and their music to the crasser
    braying of "the long-eared ass," reference not only

to his well-known disavowal of the epic form
    in favor of brevity, but also
to Tithonus, "carried off,"
    Sappho says, "to the earth's end"
        by his consort Eos, or rose-armed Dawn,
who asked Zeus to grant her lover
    immortality, forgetting to request eternal youth.

In time Tithonus withered down
    into the first cicada, which in fact
produces its distinctive sound
    not by rubbing delicate wings together, as Callimachus
    appears to have thought, but by rapidly
buckling a ribbed complex
    of membranes in its exoskeleton called timbals,

homonymic with the tall, single-headed

    drums of Brazil, redoubtable

exporter of sugar, coffee, orange juice, beef, poultry,

    and soybeans

        manipulated to withstand the complete

havoc glyphosate inflicts on every other

    plant alive that isn't likewise genetically modified

and patented, including corn, but also canola,

    alfalfa, and cotton—even glyphosate-resistant

wheat has somehow found its way

    into a field in Oregon—crops no longer

        the inheritance of all but the property of the titanic

corporation you now serve, an empire

    blowing everywhere the wind you make carries it.

•

For a purpose I hope to grow clearer in the future

    tomorrow I'll consume

        a Fritos Taco Grande BeltBuster

    at the Dairy Queen down the road from where I am.

It's been revealed to me all week on a sign.

    I've photographed

        this sign on my phone but still can't find

    any description of what it might mean

        on the internet tonight, but my guess is

it's a sandwich, likely a burger. I'll undertake this plan

maybe midafternoon, and with whatever
 nonchalance I can
  muster on what's shaping up to be
   another Texas scorcher. But no matter

 what it is, this sandwich, this burger, I know
you'll have a hand in it, especially
 if corn is present, and there's cause
to believe it must be. I think I must
 feel one way to contend with the demonic, and that's
  what you are, is to invite it
  in, take its properties on in order to know
   how better to defeat it. I think I've
been here before. I can just feel it. I can just taste
 the waste you will lay to me
bite after bite in the hot vinyl booth
 of right where you want me, calling you
  by name: Spellcaster. Fingers.
   The Great One. Rodeo. Touchdown. Wolf.

●

The way the darkness makes the stars stand out
 more intensely, appear more precisely themselves,
likewise the many
 canisters of Pringles, this entire supermarket
aisle of them, make me more humanly aware of my human
 than I know what to do with.

Nietzsche says that in order to make life bearable
    step by step the Greeks had to dream up an array
of new gods, shiningly
    exemplified by Apollo, who through ongoing
battle lays order to chaos and puts an end to the Titans'
    "divine reign of terror."

Most sources say your misuse of technology
    for destructive ends compels Zeus to deploy his
weapon of choice
    against you; others say Poseidon, your own
foster child, rises from the sea like architecture to impale
    you with the seismic

trident you forge for him; while Servius's gloss
    on Virgil's epic attributes the honor to none other
than Apollo himself
    taking the shape of the wolf in part to beautify
it from within, "as roses burst forth from the thorn-bush"
    to quote Nietzsche again

in a context different but not unrelated, like tropical
    milkweed to the native variety, whose scent
the *Times* describes as
    "sweet, spicy and ripe with an overtone of honey."
Well-meaning gardeners keep planting tropical milkweed
    in droves in their borders

to provide habitats and food for the monarch butterfly—
	who affixes her eggs to the undersides
of the milkweed's leaves
	and whose larvae eat nothing but—in hopes
of offsetting all the native plants you continue to destroy
	along the fringes of corn and soy

fields throughout the Midwest, but unlike the plainer
	native species, the tropical doesn't die back
in winter, a fact agreeable
	to monarch-infecting parasites, but flummoxing
to the monarchs themselves, many of whom,
	taken in by the luxury of a year-round milkweed supply,

end up forsaking their famous migratory flight
	to Mexico, an exercise which has come to ensure
the overall strength
	of the swarm. Enthusiasts like to call a swarm
of butterflies a "kaleidoscope," another practice which to
	my mind means well, but fails

to do justice to the monarch, in effect diminishing
	colonies that curtain fir trees in the tens of millions
per hectare into a single
	handheld toy meant to enchant the eye away
from the truth in front of it—deforestation, extreme weather,
	dozens of species lost every week.

●

From your maternal grandparents, Darkness
                              and Night,
      you inherit the knack of existing largely
                              in the figurative

but with tangible impact. Not as entities
                              with distinct
      shapes one might doodle in the margins
                              of an almanac

like Cheney's face on the body of Cthulhu,
                              but as a human
      tendency to destroy a thing as a way of
                              controlling it

and with no regard for what effects this
                              might have on
      things nearby, things over time, or things
                              not immediately

apparent, e.g., our groundwater supply—
                              which glyphosate
      snakes its way into, here and abroad, despite
                              biotech's reassurance

that the compound's slow soil mobility

                    in effect prevents

    groundwater contamination—and then

                          there's our gut flora.

    ●

Looking back, I remember the BeltBuster,

    and fondly, as comprising

        two meat patties, two cheese slices,

seasoned taco meat, Fritos, and possibly more cheese

    in a more liquid form, like a queso sauce

or its approximation, served

        on a fairly straightforward bun

    that fell apart halfway through—

        not a problem, because by that point my belt

    had, as advertised, been busted,

        again in the figurative, and I ate

with my hands what remained

    of its meat, which by that point had grown

        inseparable from the cheese,

because, as a rule of thumb, if a higher life form

    dies for my meal, I do what I can.

On the way home I tried

        for twenty minutes to photograph

    streak lightning on my phone

but failed every time, all I could capture was

a gravel road, dead and living

trees, cacti and the purple clouds

where all the lightning had been happening

and which, for Callimachus,

might call to mind the fury

of Zeus, but I thought of the comedy *The Clouds*

by Aristophanes, whose heretical

windbag depiction of Socrates—who in act 1

calls clouds "the only true gods"—

is believed to have played

a role in the philosopher's

trial and execution just shy of a quarter

century later. In *The Birth of Tragedy*

Nietzsche says Athens, mindful of the eyes

of posterity, would only have gone

so far as to punish its self-described "gadfly"

with exile, and supposes it

was Socrates himself, so tyrannically

opposed to instinct, including even

the instinct to live, who proposed his

own death as the answer to

the charges of impiety against

the city-state's gods and corruption

of its youth. What's more, Nietzsche

also says Socrates, now a daemonic force

via Euripides, was responsible

for the death of Greek tragedy,

which was once "that most magnificent temple"

and then just another pile of

rubble when what Nietzsche calls "the murderous

principle" of aesthetic Socratism,

i.e., "In order to be beautiful,

everything must be intelligible," sank

anchor in a harbor far deeper than

sense, pointed skiffs like viruses to shore

to infect dull reason into the amphitheater

where the individual, once valiant

as a golden pheasant among porcupine,

had come to face the abyss

with pleasure because it meant

constructing an illusion over it in front

of everybody, a new bridge

leading not to the conclusion the abyss

wasn't there, or wasn't real, but that it's all

that's ever either, and the truth of this

infuses the illusion with necessity.

Regarding his assessment of Socrates's

asceticism, Nietzsche may have gone a bit

overboard. It is known

that Socrates exhibited robustness
here and there, having served in three battles
as a hoplite and excelled at masonry
in his youth. He wed
Xanthippe late in life, and together
they brought three sons into a world
we might be wrong to imagine
him too eager to escape from. After

hemlock, they made him walk around
until his legs went heavy-numb.
After lying down, and as the toxin eelily
found his heart, he told his companion
Crito to remember the cock
owed to Asclepius, god of medicine. Nietzsche
interprets this as a tribute to be paid to the god
for curing him of the long sickness
of existence. More recently, Asclepius
was remembered in the plant name
Asclepias syriaca, our native milkweed.

•

Here the grasshopper Apollo says bid a hardy
welcome to the emptiness
already inside you. Sit down together
on the verandah

of coming to know it and what it will do. It will do
    what it will regardless. It is in
        your interest. Also in your interest—
    offer me beet greens on a nonreactive platter
at my temple at Delphi
    as has been customary
        for several millennia. Just make sure
that they're harvested
    at least six miles away
        from the nearest sugar beet, as all the sugar

    beets in America, which account for
roughly half your country's
    sugar production, are genetically modified
        to be glyphosate-resistant, and at a distance
less than that, transgenic contamination
    with plants in the same family,
        e.g., table beets and Swiss chard, isn't just likely,
it's inevitable.
    As for the emptiness, you can depend on it
        the way strings
            depend on the hollow body
of the guitar. I know you don't ordinarily
    trust rhetoric like that, but I see
        you have already taken my word for it.

•

One night I will walk out under a sky so clear
    I'll forget I am anywhere. The landscape won't regard

me any differently than itself—I'll be the portion of a somewhat
    greater density than beeswax, lesser when inhaling

at maximum capacity. A movement through lashes
    of wind-bent June grass; counter to the wind, but only

in velocity. That figure of the human as loge towards which
    Earth's orchestra exists to tend its point will sit

quaint then, or irrelevant, like an excavated pull-tab
    harvester ants paraded out the mouth of their habitat

in order to make life bearable. I took their photograph
    on my phone but it looks for all the world like the surface

of the moon. Then I took another of a lone jackrabbit
    I thought might be the jackrabbit I saw earlier today—

when I turned, I saw maybe a dozen jackrabbits ricochet
    into the scrub and vanish. In a way they were

all the same jackrabbit, just as I'm the same human
    they'll always run from. But we have lived too long

in the actual to let ourselves cave into the thought
    we should now try living in the abstract. There's a knot

in the wood floor where I am I keep mistaking for a scorpion.
It keeps mistaking me for Socrates, pacing the room

as we lose the feeling. But what I'm really doing is
trying to get it back, weaving to and fro if not to sweat

the toxin out, then to stage a demonstration to myself I am
alive. In the prologue to his long poem on the many

causes of what is, Callimachus says he feels mortality
sliding off him like "the three-cornered mass of Sicily."

I don't feel that. I feel malevolent forms of rationality at play.
I feel the Arctic flounder's gene sequence allowing it

to withstand frigid temperatures patched into the DNA
of flavorless tomatoes in 1991. I feel trembling in the milk

of today's goats in Utah tinkered with to produce a high-
grade spider silk for military jumpsuits. I feel the pull of Earth's

newfound moon on the aquifer beneath me and a panic
rustle wings awake on hot hexagons in Mexico, and then I

don't. But I still feel hands around my throat. I still feel
Stevens when he says: "a violence from within . . .

protects us from a violence without." I feel ribbed undersides
of milkweed's leaves and a silkiness to its parachutes

split from pods in airborne childhood. I feel at odds with
what I feel but not enough to stop. My finger in the dark

aligns the divot in the drywall with the sad last gasp of GMO-fed
catfish. I feel the sickness of existence and its portal

back in. I feel the times I walk across dissolve but I still walk.
I feel the only way to make life bearable is to make it.

JECT, THE FAMOUS GERMAN POLYMATH UNDERTOOK TO CALCULATE THE PRE
MBER OF BRICKS THE TOWER OF BABEL WOULD HAVE REQUIRED HAD IT EVER
ISHED TO QUANTIFY THE FOOLISHNESS OF THE ALREADY LONG SINCE FAILE
UCTION PROJECT, THE FAMOUS GERMAN POLYMATH UNDERTOOK TO CALCUL
CISE NUMBER OF BRICKS THE TOWER OF BABEL WOULD HAVE REQUIRED HA
R BEEN FINISHED TO QUANTIFY THE FOOLISHNESS OF THE ALREADY LONG S
LED CONSTRUCTION PROJECT, THE FAMOUS GERMAN POLYMATH UNDERTOOK
LATE THE PRECISE NUMBER OF BRICKS THE TOWER OF BABEL WOULD HAVE R

3

D IT EVER BEEN FINISHED TO QUANTIFY THE FOOLISHNESS OF THE ALREADY
CE FAILED CONSTRUCTION PROJECT, THE FAMOUS GERMAN POLYMATH UNDE
CALCULATE THE PRECISE NUMBER OF BRICKS THE TOWER OF BABEL WOULD
QUIRED HAD IT EVER BEEN FINISHED TO QUANTIFY THE FOOLISHNESS OF TH
ADY LONG SINCE FAILED CONSTRUCTION PROJECT, THE FAMOUS GERMAN POL
DERTOOK TO CALCULATE THE PRECISE NUMBER OF BRICKS THE TOWER OF BA
ULD HAVE REQUIRED HAD IT EVER BEEN FINISHED TO QUANTIFY THE FOOLIS
THE ALREADY LONG SINCE FAILED CONSTRUCTION PROJECT, THE FAMOUS GE
LYMATH UNDERTOOK TO CALCULATE THE PRECISE NUMBER OF BRICKS THE TO
BEL WOULD HAVE REQUIRED HAD IT EVER BEEN FINISHED TO QUANTIFY THE
NESS OF THE ALREADY LONG SINCE FAILED CONSTRUCTION PROJECT, THE FA
RMAN POLYMATH UNDERTOOK TO CALCULATE THE PRECISE NUMBER OF BRICK
WER OF BABEL WOULD HAVE REQUIRED HAD IT EVER BEEN FINISHED TO QUA
E FOOLISHNESS OF THE ALREADY LONG SINCE FAILED CONSTRUCTION PROJEC
MOUS GERMAN POLYMATH UNDERTOOK TO CALCULATE THE PRECISE NUMBER
CKS THE TOWER OF BABEL WOULD HAVE REQUIRED HAD IT EVER BEEN FINIS
ANTIFY THE FOOLISHNESS OF THE ALREADY LONG SINCE FAILED CONSTRUCTI
OJECT, THE FAMOUS GERMAN POLYMATH UNDERTOOK TO CALCULATE THE PRE
MBER OF BRICKS THE TOWER OF BABEL WOULD HAVE REQUIRED HAD IT EVER
ISHED TO QUANTIFY THE FOOLISHNESS OF THE ALREADY LONG SINCE FAILE
RUCTION PROJECT, THE FAMOUS GERMAN POLYMATH UNDERTOOK TO CALCUL
CISE NUMBER OF BRICKS THE TOWER OF BABEL WOULD HAVE REQUIRED HA
ER BEEN FINISHED TO QUANTIFY THE FOOLISHNESS OF THE ALREADY LONG S
LED CONSTRUCTION PROJECT, THE FAMOUS GERMAN POLYMATH UNDERTOOK
LATE THE PRECISE NUMBER OF BRICKS THE TOWER OF BABEL WOULD HAVE R
D IT EVER BEEN FINISHED TO QUANTIFY THE FOOLISHNESS OF THE ALREADY
CE FAILED CONSTRUCTION PROJECT, THE FAMOUS GERMAN POLYMATH UNDE
CALCULATE THE PRECISE NUMBER OF BRICKS THE TOWER OF BABEL WOULD
QUIRED HAD IT EVER BEEN FINISHED TO QUANTIFY THE FOOLISHNESS OF TH
ADY LONG SINCE FAILED CONSTRUCTION PROJECT, THE FAMOUS GERMAN POL

The Earth Itself

To quantify the foolishness of the already long since failed
     construction project, the famous German polymath

undertook to calculate the precise number of bricks
     the Tower of Babel would have required had it ever been

finished. The figure he came up with ran an impressive
     eighteen digits in length, climbing all the way up

to that rarely occupied hundred-quadrillions place.
     Looking at it now, between loads of laundry, the figure

calls to mind an American telephone number—area code first,
     then the prefix, then the line number, followed in turn

by a trail of eight additional zeros. I feel a little lost
     through the hypnosis of those zeros, but I still pick up

the phone and dial that number now. A recording says
     the number I've dialed isn't an actual telephone number

after all. Please try again. I do. Same result. I try dialing
     that trail of zeros instead. This time the recording says

that the call I'm making might itself be recorded. I hesitate a bit
    at the thought of that, when all this pseudoscience, all

this poking into mysteries, panting for answers, always
    harder, higher, my phone calls today and the recordings

and the laundry, the laundry—it all comes crashing down.
    I don't have time to experiment. I'm hanging up the phone.

But wait, there's more! On my rush back to the laundromat
    I remembered I forgot a part. The polymath figured out, too,

that if the tower had reached its destination, it would have
    taken over eight hundred years to climb to the top.

And further, his calculations say the mass of all those bricks
    would have outweighed, albeit slightly, the earth's own mass,

meaning the tower would have used up all the matter of
    the planet it was built on, which is foolish enough, and then

a little more, which is absurd, unless the tower is secretly
    just the earth itself, with the added weight of all the living on it.

Happiness

Even if it could be felt
all at once, instead of
in installments, instead of
this staggering
out over a lifetime
of feeling it without
warning, or even
without wanting it, seize

before sliding back
into its opposite, seismic
event, so that
by analogy, being itself
grows corrugated,
as sand does recalling
the motion of water,
or like ridges on the roof

of a good dog's mouth
science says serve
to stop the water from
escaping when lapping it

up—then again
by analogy, the feeling
of how it would feel
likewise would escape me.

Hymn to Edmond Albius

Too busy peddling my fire and trying to keep the mouths fed
and packing up belongings of the recent dead right now to access
your luxurious philosophy, though one looks forward to a time

when the universe permits, I said to my electric correspondent
who came at me puffed pink in thoughtfulness when what I needed
then as now was a quiet high enough to envision a half-gallon

brick of all-natural vanilla ice cream softening on the hot hood
of an idling cop car: the earliest rivulets, a slow loss of strict
rectangularity, then the wild gliding around on the beautiful bleak

enamel paint job as its sweet fragrance fills the air like a gift
from Madagascar I can breathe. Rapt Cortés transported cuttings
of vanilla across the Atlantic during his plunder of the Aztecs;

the Aztecs themselves fell captive to its magic after vanquishing
its first cultivators the Totonacs, who paid their conquerors tributes
of baskets stacked to heaven with cured vanilla pods like long

sentences of salutiferous essence. This is one of those instances
history likes to push your face into to try to stir your appetite
for cruelty a little, or at least make you covet the perks of it: I too

want vanilla in quantity. I want it all around me, like a fortress
of mellow dangles. It will move with me as I move and it will ward
hateful people off. For centuries Europeans tried to cultivate it

outside its native Mexico and failed. They could get the vine
to flower, but in the absence of ancestral pollinators, specifically
hummingbirds and a stingless bee, the flowers dropped off podless.

Meanwhile, Edmond Albius—born into slavery on an island
east of Madagascar known then as Bourbon, lush French colony
and home to roses, home to one active volcano, one dormant, and one

arena-like caldera that holds the record for most rainfall shed
in one location by a single tropical cyclone ever, namely Hyacinthe—
knew enough from orchids at age twelve in 1841 to think to lift

with a bamboo splint the flap of the rostellum dividing the pollen-
heavy male anther from the female stigma in order to rub the pollen
on the stigma's eager wand. Within weeks the pods had begun

to form and lengthen into joyous beanlike squiggles laden with
tiny seeds like secrets of the universe as Albius at the shore and under
bright southern stars breathed out I hope in a kind of enlargement

akin to liberty from time, so that on that occasion he might feel
briefly as if his own, even as his method of vanilla pollination
belonged first to his master, then Madagascar, and then the world,

with nearly all vanilla produced today as Albius taught us, including

the kind in Breyers since 1866, fourteen years before Albius died

unrecognized, in poverty, in misery to be exact, while everyone white

around him grew rich with vanilla, adding it to candy, Coca-Cola,

Chanel No. 5, and even in effigy to the air freshener dangling

down in my Uber, its waves whispering Albius, Albius, but inaudibly.

Escape into Time

Back where the start was
in time I came to feel, before
or without any basic understanding,
the hands holding me down
wanted likewise to reassure me
there was no place other
than right where I was kept:
chair, table, void-side window

overlooking the nothingness
and the hands that held me there
must have held me without
understanding in time
I would come to feel to keep me
implied other places must likewise
exist, otherwise what
was I kept from to begin with,

and by extension, everywhere
apart from where the hands were
congealed into one
comprehensive elsewhere, all time
not the present became one time,
and even when denied

any movement not a form
of leaning forward, nonetheless

I arrived at the border of
all other places every time at once,
so that to hold out my hand
would bring it no closer
to the garment of my caretaker
than to the first known garment
of its kind, or to the hand
that designed it, or to the hand of

the godhead etching into stone,
a stone rolled back from
the mouth of a tomb, or the mouth
of a painter of clock faces
numbering the void with light
steps around a pit the uranium rises
out of like a crib in Colorado
where a dirt path into the endless

distance erases itself as I too
will erase myself when I take it
the way I always have
reverberating inwardly, a machine
through time, each future inescapably
historical, but I am traveling
back where the start was
not yet waiting for me all along.

Traveler

Admittedly, there have been times, as after antihistamines
    and a lager at the airport bar, when I can make like

I belong here, minding my own carry-on behind me
    like the nonchalant, buoyed through a mount in cheer

or cheerfulness I can't call false, or can but just plain
    don't, my fixity dissolving like some paper boat on blue

carpet scrolling down the gate and aisle, shoulders brushed
    to others' gently, neighborlike, and often, and as if

I hadn't noticed, but I do, it is my task. A sudden flash
    of what might happen when it did, but days ago, and then

the rope of calm around my neck again, I settle in my seat,
    a window in the back, and pray to what I pay for,

which is an empty sky, or else a cloud in what appears
    to be the center of the sky, to feel the fade of what I only

recently eased into, this lack of history between us
    making it all the easier. (I think I hadn't expected life

to be kind to me, not in light of the pounding of it, so I must have
    thought I could trick it, lead it into thinking I wasn't

really there. Later on, I think I changed my mind, but by
    then it was too late.)

                  Gone forward, pulling it off

but awkwardly, timed as if time's artichoke had wept in
    front of me in the white kitchen, or on a pond on which

intoned a lotus, then a moon; greased in plenitude, up to
    and including—then all its little hands, which knit

a lifework out of hours, days; centuries unstuck like yellow
    vinyl from the tabletop, the noise of it so common-

place we didn't notice it, or when we did, we let it pass
    by tacitly as nails until all the landscapes they held up

dropped out of custody, and now it can't be heard again.
    Or say the flatness of the tabletop were the known

universe, all of it, and I'm just a random smirch residing
    in the northeast corner, comparable to many other smirches,

nothing special, until I vanish from this flatness into another
    layer of it, into depth. We might think of it as traveling

under the table, but the smirches, who only experience
  flatness, know no under. They only know that I was there

and then I wasn't. And when I resurface in an instant
  somewhere in the south, it's still just an instant to me,

but to the others, who are nowhere to be found, it was an instant
  three hundred years in the past.

                              White birches lean

through a mist like plastic drinking straws, the same
  kind a tribesman from Papua New Guinea once drove

through the hole in his septum in lieu of the traditional
  wooden spoke or bone. The anthropologist in the back of

the room cried. She had seen the documentary many times before
  but still cried. She sensed in this image the collapse

of a culture, its unstoppable tumbling into the corporate
  fast-food abyss. I could see this. At the same time I couldn't

look up into his face and make myself see anything less
  or more than a person, one with the capacity to choose

or choose not to do what he had done. I knew I had to
  be wrong. I knew I should want him not to choose what

he possibly only appeared to have chosen, meaning external
        forces might have compelled him to take up the straw

instead of materials his ancestors used, but I couldn't distinguish
        between wanting this and wanting to preserve him

in time like an object, even if to do so meant denying him
        his ability to choose, permitting him only to do to his face

what left Baltimore comfortable.

                                        Anyone moves through
        days less than completely, the washing of dishes

start to finish, water half-scalding the hands so the feet
        don't remember events that the land underneath

them supported, a hope for gain so consistent in the humus
        it becomes for us an unavoidable drink, the whole

crow family chuffing overhead as we trust our taproots
        to skirt the bad aquifer. Anyone oftener in the soft-

scented borders abuzz beside museum doors will anchor
        thoughts elsewhere than in insects on whose loud labor

we depend unendingly. As for me, I like to think of myself as able
        to function at a certain level, equipped to walk among

a company of bees at ease with my place in an ancient
    relation, a live participant in a pattern whose longevity

is a thing of beauty, admiring our symbiosis in Sunday
    sun as an abstract love with benefits, but then I think

we'd cloud them in a stink of toxins if they didn't pollinate
    the fruit we ate or vomit honey, and they don't think

of us at all, they're too busy, or aren't equipped to, or don't
    see the point, if there is any.

                    Half-aware in the dark

air above New York, a common swift, known to doze in flight
    the way a dolphin does through the sea, one hemi-

sphere of its brain set to slow-wave sleep while the other
    maintains vigilance, the inner eye of us widening

as it beams back and forth godlike across the soft office
    floor of our experience, the outer and inner divisions of it

parted by a cleft that looks from this height like nothing
    but a papercut, I drop in on red activity filed in the

fourth quadrant outer division, labyrinth of mismanagement
    as far as the eye can see, its index cards alone the size

of antlers on Irish elk, which is to say so large they prevent
    successful completion of "the normal business of life,"

I've heard it said, or else it was just some idea I had
    once about futility in a bathtub, but when I reach out

to grab the file, having been lowered down to the air-
    space just above it, the antiquated suspension system up

and reverses, hauling me backward through the element
    I belong to, torn as if from the hand that would spare me

the burden of remembering.

                    Nothing to be afraid of but
    nothing now, a light-absorbing liquid tucked behind a dam

constantly wanting to unknit itself, thinking to fail by plan
    might be better than to succeed for a stretch through

violent worry, only to fail in time anyway; you sat beside me
    on the green chair, birdlike, fidgeting in your girlhood

as we read together from a magazine, facts about the lives
    of honeybees, nothing to be afraid of: to generate,

on average, a single pound of honey, a colony has to draw
    nectar from two million flowers, or enough red roses

to send a dozen red roses to every resident of Columbia, Mo.
  And to visit all those flowers, the colony has to fly,

collectively, fifty thousand miles, over one-fifth the distance
  from the earth to the moon, which holds our thoughts

in place if we have nowhere else to place them, as when
  we read the average worker bee, in all its lifetime, will only

produce one-twelfth a teaspoon of honey, meaning that I
  have stirred the lifework of a dozen bees into my teacup

thoughtlessly, a devourer of lifeworks, this present only
  one example, I turn my head away.

                              Awake again in under-

brush, helmet of scrub pine and sassafras, an earth beneath
  my hooved feet elastic with its mosses, I walk out

to the human clearing, late winter, under a surplus of stars.
  Gently, neighborlike, my animal ear upheld against

the wigwam, the stripped-bark sides of it like the surface
  of a rumored planet, discernible at last in the late winter

sky that appears, as noted, invested with more stars
  than necessary, although necessity would seem to have

no place in the matter, and it must be I who has imported it.
   In the firelight the colonist feeds the dying sachem

fruit preserves with a blunt English knife, nursing him back
   to health, and it's my task to determine, through

the tension of the wigwam, whether he performs this
   kindness out of love, strategy, or else some mixture of

the two, and if this last, I am asked to determine whether
   the two feelings stay distinct in the mixture, or do

they fuse, and if the latter, what known apparatus might
   best take the measure, or what new one might we devise,

and is it love-strategy then, or strategy-love, is one half
   always stronger, or is it not like that at all.

                                    When I fly

back to where I'm from, or feel I must be, will I be thought
   a failure to the others there, because I am, but only

in the strict sense, having failed to accomplish what I felt
   I had been asked to, which was to undertake what

can't in fact be done, not the way we had been made to
   think we might be able to. That was our mistake, if we were

more than one. If not, then it was mine. I worry that
    I won't be able, in the strict sense, to make the others

see the beauty of it, all of it, which I admit I can only
    see in part, even after lifelong travels, and then I think,

this must be what they want, for me to return incapable,
    brokener, insisting on the beauty of what can't be

understood, not the way we thought, and they, if more
    than one, will welcome me, nodding in time like the holy

entities on a diptych, and if otherwise, I will be there
    to becalm myself, and to be the ship I wait for, and the ocean

will be ocean, no matter how I cross it, and late winter
    sky will still be sky, until there's no ship left to wait for.

Jonah

If I don't speak to
the darkness it
swallows me.

The Death of Print Culture

There's a sort of meteorologist
Jeremy Jacoby Joffrey Jagger Josh
that likes to make a show
of his sensitivity in the hopes of
winning the favor of strong
female onlookers, particularly those
who resemble his primary
care physician, and watching it
"all play out on the screen"
my friends, it is like watching
Storm Spencer Pomponius Vince
an anthropomorphized pistachio
ice-cream cone incrementally
baring its pale ass to a category-

five hurricane, which is not to
comment on the conduct
of meteorologists categorically
or to compare them all
to cartoon food or strong women to
dangerous weather, it's just that
increasingly there are all
these sensitive meteorologists

Connor Conover Constantine Wolf
peering through their tears
to notice the anchor tilting her
head noticeably as if to measure
a previously undetected depth
when in truth she is remembering

a rapidly bitten-into falafel
sandwich falling apart all over
our nation's leading news periodical
dampening gloss pages
as she wonders if she should just
throw it into the trash or else
surreptitiously return it to
the stack of other periodicals
compromised by happenstance
in the network kitchenette,
wash hands with rose geranium
foaming hand soap and call it a day
but not once does she ever
consider taking it home with her.

The Death of the Author

One warm Good Friday after having fasted
I rode my azure Huffy to Benny's Home & Auto

2.5 miles away with David Simoneau
for what I can't remember, a good deal farther

than ever before, much less on a rumbling
holy empty stomach, and the strange air turned

impatient with me, palpable, and the new-tire smell
of small business blurred my vision

in from the edges as I walked automatic
to the sliding door but missed, banging pins

and needles of my face against the plate-
glass window, dying in public the first time ever

backwards for a minute on the rutted welcome mat
till flights of angels did around me sing

He's on drugs is what he is, but all I was
was Catholic. As for drugs, some years later

for all I could tell I was dead again all over
on Scott and Kathy's bathroom tile with a stone-

cold paralysis I still access on occasion
as I wish, only this time I was shall we say

eager to be revived, and then the green foil
cylindrical canister of Comet scouring powder

told me to muster all my strength and hurl it
down the hall in an arc like the celestial

object from which our product draws its name
whereupon rescuers would come the way the magi

came to the Christ child guided by a star.
Lynn was dead too but probably remembers it

differently than I. Something tells me for a time
I might have been torn between the Comet and Kathy's

marquetry jewelry box, which would have been
too personal a sacrifice so I'm happy to say

I chose the cleanser in the end, not that marquetry
for all its repulsive involvement and dizzy

suggestiveness of hands isn't almost always better off
destroyed, at least to someone whose most vivid

if not earliest association with hands is
about which probably the less said the better,

but between these deaths I was in fact killed
on the regular, over and over, albeit in the iffy

safety of a home, where the dead in time mistook
me for one of them, or to put it accurately

came to know and stand around the bed of,
intending then, I thought, to terrorize me more

but since the art of what went down is left
mine to decipher, I say what they did was keep

part of me alive, wrapping it in the plastic of
cloud architecture, for some other world than this.

The Death of Truth

The world is a horrible place. —Think Big, Donald Trump

But my own value fluctuates, falling up and down
with the markets and with attitudes and with feelings,
even my own feelings, but I try. Studies have shown

how I try. The sheer force of numbers. The ceiling
shakes with it, which only goes to show—all the science
is on my side. If I want more, I put an order in. I sing

the body mac and cheese, deep-fried: Tom Jefferson's
personal recipe. But we improved it, like the Taj Mahal.
Eighth wonder of the world. Dot my i's in diamonds

and that's what I am. Handsomest Cobb salad of them all.
Ty Cobb himself told me so. Roseanne is my witness.
A very nice letter. I haven't opened it. A good call

with no obstruction whatsoever. Legs like a gymnast
from here to Venus. Should put the best possible spin on it.
If it's organized, it isn't crime anymore, it's business.

Gather round now, real estate. Come and make a planet
real again. Bible says Ananias sold a spot of property
to make a cash gift to the apostles, which was unfortunate.

Not a good idea. They didn't have it in their mentality
to deal with the art of it. The whole idea of personal
ownership made Paul nervous. Guy just wasn't ready.

Don't get me wrong: this isn't me. Ananias set a small
portion aside for himself, for family. Nothing you or I
wouldn't do. When he handed his gift to Paul, Paul

wasn't too happy. He asked where the rest was and why
Ananias let the devil take up residence in his heart.
The devil rents. That's what I'm hearing. He said to lie

about this is to lie not to him, but to the Holy Spirit,
and boom! Ananias bit it. Dropped dead on the carpet or
probably dirt floor at this point. If it's me, I like carpet,

but that's just me. Did I say Paul? It was Peter. Peter,
Paul. Same difference. Either way, they dragged the guy's
wife in next and put her to the test. Didn't do any better.

Also dead, also on the floor. The moral of the story is:
Don't give anything away. Only acquire. Lie constantly to
lie better, live longer. Charge the devil through the nose

to pitch tent in your heart. What you can't get, disvalue
loudly in public. Not worth anything, like safety pins.
No thank you. Only losers need those, losers like that blue

cartoon do-nothing donkey. A tail like that and no one's
taking you seriously. Hold yourself like artwork till you're
golden. Art lies all the time, and look: nothing happens.

November Paraphrase

What I meant was that I still wasn't sure, and then a wave
in the literal sense rerouted much of my attention
from the matter at hand, which had come to have to do
with getting on in spite of everything, meaning whatever
lay ahead of us, especially in light of what we felt we knew
we wanted of a life, or from it, not only for ourselves
but as much for other persons now, including numbers
we might name, and then the rest we could only imagine

giving, somehow, name to. It's hard to put a finger on
what it is about the ocean, how it always wants me
dead, specifically on its floor, with all my earthly assets
weaving in it lazily, as if some nightclub compliment
paid one celebrity to another, but that's a big part of it
right there—all that rhetoric, desire, on whose leash a person
steps into the mouth of power, all the while trusting
we only ever gain from it. What I meant was that I still

wasn't sure, here without embellishment, even after
time had passed for clarification, having left it as much
a feeling now as a thought, which no doubt made it easier
for one gray disturbance in a field of like disturbances

to cash in on what grew tender. Simply stated, there was no
other way to put it, or none I couldn't easily dismiss
as approximate, and so I did, the way a gull huddled into
its breast on a pylon is often regarded as a monument

to oneself. Not that I didn't correct it but for a duration
it had been real. That feeling. Which isn't to say that
I, too, wanted me dead, or at least no longer existing as I
had appeared to up until that point, although the evidence
inches toward that notion at the same rate as the text
at the bottom of my television, which is to say in the way
we've all been buffeted by a force only to parse it as opposite
to what we intend, which I take to be best expressed

by not answering the question, a form of protection from
error and its wind, again like the gull, but only insofar as
getting on in this regard—in violent abeyance, uncertain as
what we did, or rather didn't do, did its harm to those
we named ourselves as much to those we can only imagine
the planet on behalf of—can ever be correct, when in practice,
what it is, though hard to put a finger on, is like stepping
back into the mouth of power, having taken it for your own.

NyQuil

Everyone had been going on about the wind
and what in the world they were planning to do about it.
Some had decided to make large plastic shields
to relieve themselves of its various effects

while others surrendered to it readily, opening up
all their windows and doors and just letting it
have its way with them. To these I gave my admiration;
to the others, my respect. But is there nothing

in between, I asked, conveying myself to the couch
as one might assist a visitor of great wisdom
and delicacy across a divide, a contemplative type—
which I had theretofore not known myself to be.

How long I must have slept there, how deeply . . .
Once in a dream I laid hands on a shield of bronze
with silver inlay, emblazoned with the head of a fox,
but woke instead to find them reaching out

for the window and ready to open it. Only by then
the wind had stopped, and there was no one anywhere
to go on with. For a calm had overtaken the air.
The long blue calm about which nothing can be said.

Leviathan

My citizenship is most acutely
felt at night when I entrust myself

into the dark and sulfury confusion
of the belly of it, having already

submitted to a long lick of the just
barely visible mucus of its laws,

whose warm coat protects me from
the perilous storm, the numerous

nocturnal forms, and much anxiety
regarding same, which would otherwise

do enormous harm were it not for
the double capsule that seals me off

from it, from other, from self, and in
the good night's sleep that leaves

me waking sticky with indebtedness
but prepared to join the workforce.

Mutual Life

Sometimes there's a person who pretends to be talking
to another person or maybe he'll just pretend to be
talking to an idea or object as if it were a person
but in truth he's not really talking to anyone or

-thing—he's not even talking to himself, he's only
writing. We pretend not to notice. Sometimes who writes
writes he hasn't been able to write much lately
and that it's only with great difficulty he is able to

write this now. He writes he holds the personification
of his capacity or drive to write responsible for
all this recent difficulty, addressing his complaint
to the personification directly, asking how could she

be so cruel, how could she just take off like that
when there was still so much work to do, work he can't
imagine getting on with without her hand in his.
The personification can't respond independent of

the writer who in turn can't articulate her response
unless she lets him. The faint mechanical clicking
that falls between thoughts as if to link them together is
inopportune. The tension between the two half-repels,

half-magnetizes. This makes things a little awkward
for the rest of us. There must be some slack bungalow
he thinks where the personifications go to smash
up against each other, testing out boundaries to come

to know themselves better but then they just get too
ridiculous with it, he can see it now—how they stretch
out so indiscriminately that by the time they're up
for coming home they're not what we want anymore.

Or not a bungalow so much as a kind of brown-scented
common area that our figments nest in temporarily
to pursue the material fantasies we hatch for them
in spite of ourselves. Either way, the one who writes

pretending to speak to one who isn't wants to honor
the particular beauty of what is, knowing all the while
beauty fades in tiny increments and sometimes even
great big leaps that in another context might be thought

achievements, noting to honor in this instance means
to construct a form for far beyond the mutability
dogging every example of terrestrial perfection, up to
and including the programmatically celebrated diamond

which is itself no less subject to the laws of physics
than the daffodil or macaroon or fennec fox, but for which
infinitely more human examples have been maimed
and killed. Again we approach it: the brink of thinking

about the consequences of our taste for perfection only
to back away from it again fast, almost as if away
reflected an authority or some clear wisdom distilled
from our forebears' raw experience, akin to our obedience

to colonial handrails, routes, or something else entirely
humming in the walls. We feel the phantom hand of culture
rest consolingly on our shoulder the minute before it
thwacks us on the ass or undertakes the long invasive

surgery we can feel but were supposed to be asleep for.
But say who writes is sad. And saddened genuinely
not by the staged betrayal of someone he only pretends to
be speaking to and saddened not by the condition of

his tender love which also seems at least a little phony
but saddened instead by the terms of what must
be called his life. The inevitable trash of it and all
he might be thought to value. He advocates so loudly

for the transportability of the beauty of the love object
into the realm of art for safekeeping we almost fail
to recall how he kicked things off by accusing his own
personal ambassador from that realm, no less an ideal

version of the temporary, of having not only changed
but of having been debased—of having wanted it, even.
His loudness can only cover up so much. Nothing can
escape decay. He has to know this. He has to know that

his art can only preserve what's real rhetorically, and yet
he concludes by urging the personification to render
the love object and all its beauty past corruption and up
into fame as she mobilizes the public against the cold

campaign of time. We see the broad snowy battlefield
demarcated from the rote of the world by a parenthesis
of trees, its balance of deciduous and evergreen varieties
suggestive of the American North as well as of death

and immortality, respectively. We see the still profile of
the general training off into the distance as she waits
forever for the arrival of an enemy who is always already
everywhere anyway, her soldiers armed with nothing

more than figures of speech. We think the whole tableau
refers to what hangs statistically in the lobby of any
city's life insurance company to distract clients from the fact
of an impending doom. (In time the untouched expanse

will bear the marks of those who came in snow to fight
and went or fell, their bloody footprints an index not only
of their comings and goings but of hopes, thoughts,
and familial tics as well.) The mausoleal grandeur of this

revivalist architecture helps, too. At some point who writes
separates from the rest of us to test the lobby's bronze
revolving door designed in 1888 right here in Philadelphia
to infuse one's oneness with mechanical replaceability.

Sometimes the final cause of what we make turns out
not to reveal itself until it's put to use. Sometimes we think
we're pretending to talk but what we're really doing is
trying not to die. What words we use are determined by

the burrito bowl we ate for lunch, the rustling in the hedges
passed along the way, or the false-fresh urban air in which
one feels the great relief of having just disbanded from
a team whose objective came to appear to be the development

of new ways to befuddle through the asking of questions.
We're befuddled enough already, thanks. But we forgive you.
Who writes, we forgive you. Figures of speech, forebears,
impending doom, we forgive you. Now get out of the way.

LIVE IN IT HAPPILY, THEN I'LL BE HAPPY NEVER TO LIVE IN IT HAPPILY AG

S TRUE THAT A PERSON HAS TO BECOME MORE THAN HALF-DEAD TO THIS WO

E IN IT HAPPILY, THEN I'LL BE HAPPY NEVER TO LIVE IN IT HAPPILY AGAIN

S TRUE THAT A PERSON HAS TO BECOME MORE THAN HALF-DEAD TO THIS WO

E IN IT HAPPILY, THEN I'LL BE HAPPY NEVER TO LIVE IN IT HAPPILY AGAIN

S TRUE THAT A PERSON HAS TO BECOME MORE THAN HALF-DEAD TO THIS WO

E IN IT HAPPILY, THEN I'LL BE HAPPY NEVER TO LIVE IN IT HAPPILY AGAIN

S TRUE THAT A PERSON HAS TO BECOME MORE THAN HALF-DEAD TO THIS WO

E IN IT HAPPILY, THEN I'LL BE HAPPY NEVER TO LIVE IN IT HAPPILY AGAIN

S TRUE THAT A PERSON HAS TO BECOME MORE THAN HALF-DEAD TO THIS WO

4

E IN IT HAPPILY, THEN I'LL BE HAPPY NEVER TO LIVE IN IT HAPPILY AGAIN

S TRUE THAT A PERSON HAS TO BECOME MORE THAN HALF-DEAD TO THIS WO

E IN IT HAPPILY, THEN I'LL BE HAPPY NEVER TO LIVE IN IT HAPPILY AGAIN

S TRUE THAT A PERSON HAS TO BECOME MORE THAN HALF-DEAD TO THIS WO

E IN IT HAPPILY, THEN I'LL BE HAPPY NEVER TO LIVE IN IT HAPPILY AGAIN

S TRUE THAT A PERSON HAS TO BECOME MORE THAN HALF-DEAD TO THIS WO

E IN IT HAPPILY, THEN I'LL BE HAPPY NEVER TO LIVE IN IT HAPPILY AGAIN

S TRUE THAT A PERSON HAS TO BECOME MORE THAN HALF-DEAD TO THIS WO

E IN IT HAPPILY, THEN I'LL BE HAPPY NEVER TO LIVE IN IT HAPPILY AGAIN

S TRUE THAT A PERSON HAS TO BECOME MORE THAN HALF-DEAD TO THIS WO

E IN IT HAPPILY, THEN I'LL BE HAPPY NEVER TO LIVE IN IT HAPPILY AGAIN

S TRUE THAT A PERSON HAS TO BECOME MORE THAN HALF-DEAD TO THIS WO

E IN IT HAPPILY, THEN I'LL BE HAPPY NEVER TO LIVE IN IT HAPPILY AGAIN

S TRUE THAT A PERSON HAS TO BECOME MORE THAN HALF-DEAD TO THIS WO

E IN IT HAPPILY, THEN I'LL BE HAPPY NEVER TO LIVE IN IT HAPPILY AGAIN

S TRUE THAT A PERSON HAS TO BECOME MORE THAN HALF-DEAD TO THIS WO

VE IN IT HAPPILY, THEN I'LL BE HAPPY NEVER TO LIVE IN IT HAPPILY AGAIN

S TRUE THAT A PERSON HAS TO BECOME MORE THAN HALF-DEAD TO THIS WO

VE IN IT HAPPILY, THEN I'LL BE HAPPY NEVER TO LIVE IN IT HAPPILY AGAI

S TRUE THAT A PERSON HAS TO BECOME MORE THAN HALF-DEAD TO THIS WO

VE IN IT HAPPILY, THEN I'LL BE HAPPY NEVER TO LIVE IN IT HAPPILY AGAI

S TRUE THAT A PERSON HAS TO BECOME MORE THAN HALF-DEAD TO THIS W

VE IN IT HAPPILY, THEN I'LL BE HAPPY NEVER TO LIVE IN IT HAPPILY AGAI

S TRUE THAT A PERSON HAS TO BECOME MORE THAN HALF-DEAD TO THIS W

VE IN IT HAPPILY, THEN I'LL BE HAPPY NEVER TO LIVE IN IT HAPPILY AGAI

'S TRUE THAT A PERSON HAS TO BECOME MORE THAN HALF-DEAD TO THIS W

Lycopodium Obscurum

If it's true that a person has to become more than half-
    dead to this world to live in it happily, then I'll be happy
never to live in it happily again. Let the phenomena
    alternately capsize and crank me up into the Atlantic

air—I will hang there jangling till the point of view
    turns out to be borne on the concave back of some far
too faulty conception of happiness, which is to say just
    say the word and I'll tear it down and get back to work.

Here in my dirt laboratory, here where I take my time
    and have it, what shatters on the workbench wends its way
to the floor in light-feathered sentences whose truth
    content amounts to as much as the average rainfall

between syllables in *silver.* Sentences that chirp insights
    back and forth nights like peckish metaphysicists
united over pastry, an altarpiece of it, baroque in an effort
    to avoid further scrutiny of the universal diagram

for the formation of questions regarding every possible
    proposition. Having only recently tattooed it to the taut
backs of truffle hogs we then released into the autumn
    of their abutting acreage to no avail, I can't fault them.

They can't be faulted. Not entirely. Not when the need
    to articulate their quest in material terms animates limbs
no less than hungers of the body. But something keeps
    going wrong, something that calls for cold long walks

through quiet acreage. A chance to glimpse, as in time-
    lapse photography, the pert tassels of what's classified
as a fern ally insist through the topsoil. I never knew
    its binomial till long after the woods in which it grew

got axed to pay for my tutorials. Wee ranch-style houses
    fortify that land now, habitats where lives like mine
go drab between lasagna and last month's crossword puzzles.
    Dust descends on candy dishes. Radon detectors blink

plainly in the basements. The sentences want to know
    how much of what they perceive is actually a message.
Sorry. I stand corrected. What they really want to know
    is how much of what they perceive is actually a pastry.

Pretty much all of it, I say. After so many failed strivings
    into darkness, into ether, they've come to value most
what they can lay their hands on, place inside their mouths.
    All that animus spent hunting the intrinsic instead of

honing methods to evaluate the relative wore them out.
    Go to bed, little sentences. The ghosts of club moss rise
up because I've felt them here. I tend to them this way,
    a member of their movement. And maybe what irrupts

calls for that. For less gridwork and more choreography,
     for a form including time, change, and not just setting into
fixed position—although back in the day the sentences
     would've wagered all dance had gridwork hidden in it.

Tonight I'll board the ship with caution because it is too
     dark now not to, hands on the rope rail, eyes on my feet up
the gangplank and back against the stars beneath which
     happiness will be thought the motion of a mind whereby

a value is performed. Like a show of respect for the forest
     that startles us into feeling at home being lost in it. Insofar as
this position can only be borne on the back of a somewhat
     loose conception of feeling, I am starting a new way to feel.

Lapis Lazuli

A finger of light
shed from the North Star
tapped my forehead
as I slept,
repeating a vehicle
is no one single
part of itself, it isn't

even the sum
of its parts, it's how
its parts relate and how
this fits
the common idea of
what a vehicle is
meant to be and do.

I wake to find I am
engulfed
entirely in blue, but safe
inside
my vehicle, and how
its parts relate
is what the ocean

is to air, or tears are

to the dew.

I read the wolf has no

concept of the unsayable.

It meant one thing

at the time, but

now it means another.

Levitation

Apart from loved ones' speech, the plonk of a wild blueberry
into an empty plastic bucket at the end of July will be the sound

I console myself with as I die again this time in the soundlessness
of deep space. Time runs out. That's what it does. I remember

a kind scorch of sun, small-scented autumn clematis, old oak
overhanging my room like the grandparent who couldn't exactly

protect me but had to know what I had to feel. Head on my pillow
certain what was real was thinking, and everything external was

just practice. But there were times, places that did come close
to a completeness, close enough. The blueberry bushes burning

red as brushfire come October under wide cyan sky: early on I felt
most welcome where alone. When the planet dies, it dies despite

and because of human feeling. Hope, sorrow; anger, greed. I never
did grow comfortable with it: splintered glass around my feet

and nuclear terror, the loudness of near people in chemical distress
needing to express it over and over, weaponizing the language

at me as I waited for the beams of light to break through birches
heralding my departure. And not sunbeams, either, but beams

from the gold oblong vehicle all of us saw once interrupting kickball.
Why make a person see something so exceptional if it won't be

central to their life. Why only this one way of it we fight for
and only when there's profit. The light, the light. I feared I might

lift above the parish muttering into mass, an arrogance I forgive
of a child: primary narcissism has its time, place. But a superpower

can't depend on stunting everyone into it interminably and still
expect to progress. Yesterday I walked my darkening circles sick

of how ashamed I felt of everything but sunflowers. Tonight I feel
alright. The light, the light, the light. But what I want to feel is

like Teresa, ground to pieces, hopelessly elect: as I try to create
resistance, it will feel as though some great force beneath my feet

pushes me up, pushes me along the way a disk hovers in the air
through clouds and over oak, over dogwood and the basketball hoop,

the cold magnetic pull of Earth neutralized by an equal force
acting in opposition, Earth's magnetic current measured, analyzed

and overtaken, forcing a body into space: breath held, counting down
by halves eternally, Earth a memory, weight no intrinsic property

of matter, matter inessential to reason, no reason needed to support
flight: nothing visible, nothing tangible, nothing audible, nothing more.

Some Comforts at the Expense of Others

I dreamed of home invasion, and of a great celebrity
hidden inside a series of rooms, each hermetically
separated by glossy, voice-activated doors, each
bordered on both sides by facsimile rooms, identical

to the real room in every detail, which were in turn
separated from the next room's facsimile by a sort of
hybrid non-room, its decor partaking of elements
of the two facsimile rooms it served to divide, or rather

of the two real rooms the facsimiles referred to.
Only a verified member of the household could tell
the real room from its two facsimiles, but it was unclear
whether this was due to long exposure, microchip

technology, or the receptivity to signs of life so small
only very hungry or frightened people sense them.
Now in midseason, it is apparent that these non-rooms,
separating one facsimile from the next, breed distinct

moods and possibilities, just as brackish habitats
like deltas, marshes, some lochs and coastal lagoons
inaugurate and foster a plenitude of life forms neither
purely fresh nor purely salt water alone can sustain.

In the confessional, the celebrity appeared to regret
the existence of the non-rooms, deposited as they were
with a ghostliness and quotient of blue found nowhere else,
observing that no verified member of the household

would ever choose to enter them, much less spend
disposable time in them in the cold. This would signal
something was amiss, some danger at hand, possibly
an invasion, and possibly from within, like the buildup

of urate crystals in a big toe, or slight myopia due
to highly reflective skin, or else a simple, seamlessly
engineered distraction, personified through the dream as
an influencer in athleisure remarking on the vertigo

of watching on one's phone a video of small children
being lowered down by bucket into a dark toxic tunnel
near the border of oblivion to retrieve some fraction
of the cobalt in the battery of the privilege to feel nothing.

Poem Interrupted by Whitesnake

That agreeable feeling you haven't been able to
put into words to your satisfaction despite
too many white-knuckled attempts to do so might

prove in the end to be nothing more than
satisfaction itself, an advanced new formula
just waiting like product to be marketed as such:

Let my logo be the couch, I can feel it pulse
as the moon like a fool I have come to feel attached to
continues to pull back an estimated 1.6 inches

every solar year, *Let my logo be the couch*
you merge into nights until you can't
rise like the shadows in a factory warehouse

in historic Secaucus built on top of old swamp-
land I can feel it: *Let my logo be the couch*
you merge into nights until you can't remember

what you wanted to begin with. Let my theme
be the turning of an infinite catalogue's waterlogged
pages over again till what you wanted finds you

widened in the air above the city as a goldfinch,
state bird of New Jersey, stops midflight and falls
to the asphalt of a Walmart parking lot. Where it lands

is a sacred site, and Earth is covered in them,
each opening an eye within whose whorl
a wheat field generates. As this happens inside

oneself, one has felt oneself to be owner of it.
From the perimeter, quiet, you are watching over
a beelike harmony of workers busy with their tasks:

some cut the wheat, others bundle it; others picnic
in the shade of a laden pear tree, itself a form of
labor, too, unfolding at the worksite, a gentle

pride gilding observation like jellied sunlight
spread through October. And because it happens
right inside you, you feel you must be the owner of it,

owner at least of what you feel, but when you call out to
the workers, even kindly, they won't call back
in kind, they won't even look up from their work.

There must be someplace

else where life takes place besides in front of
merchandise, but at the moment I can't think of it.

In the clean white light of the market I am where
  I appertain, where everything exists for me

to purchase. If there's a place of not meaning
  what you feel but at the same time meaning every

trembly word, or almost, I might have been taught
  better to avoid it, but
            here I go again

on my own, going down the only road I've ever
  known, trusting Secaucus's first peoples

meant something specific and true when they fused
  the words *seke*, meaning *black*, and *achgook*,

meaning *snake*, together to make a compound
  variously translated as "place where the snake

hides," "place of black snakes," or, simply,
  "salt marsh."
            Going moon over the gone marsh

Secaucus used to be, I keep making the same
  mistake over and over, and so do you, gradually

speeding up your orbital velocity, and thereby
  increasing your orbital radius, just like Kepler

said you would—and though I keep trying not
    to take it to heart, I can't see where else there is

to go with it. In German, a *Kepler* makes hoods
    like those the workers wear who bundle twigs

for kindling under irregular gloom. One looks as if
    about to make repairs to a skeletal umbrella

or to thoughts a windmill might entertain by means
    of a silver fish. Off in the distance, ships tilt

up the choppy inlet. Often when I look all the way
    at a given object, I feel it looking back, evaluating

my capacity to afford it.
                  Maybe not wanting
    anything in particular leaves you mildly

wanting whatever, constantly, spreading like a wheat
    field inside you as far as the edge of the pine

where the real owners hunt fox. They keep you
    believing everything you see and feel are actually

yours or yours to choose. And maybe it's this
    belief that keeps you from burning it all down.

In this economy, I am like the fox, my paws no good
for fire-starting yet, and so I scamper back

to my deep den to fatten on whatever I can find.
Sated, safe, disremembering what it's like

up there, meaning everywhere, I tuck nose under tail
after I exhaust the catalogues, the cheap stuff,

and sad talk to the moon, including some yelping
but never howling at it, which is what a wolf does.

Poem on a Stair

On every stairway
    with the kite-shaped step
I stop on that step
    one second
to commemorate
one particular step
    in the shape of a kite
I'll never again
    be able to step on

I'll never again
    be able to set foot on
one particular
    step in the shape
of a kite
but there's reason to think
    it still exists
albeit no longer
    for me to step on

Low light, obsidian,
    Florida water, cedar-
wood cone—

I will never again
set foot on the one
step in the flesh
    but when I step on another
like it, it's as if
    I'm stepping on

Low light, obsidian,
    seashell lined
in mother-of-pearl, to set
    foot on the one
is to step on the other
now, long ago—
    blown sheets in the wind,
a railing I can feel
    the absence supper.

Poem Written with a Pinecone in My Hand

Here in my hand a cone from the beautiful eastern white pine sits
an offering from the tree planted thirty years ago after earth softened up
come spring enough to dig a hole roughly twice the size of the burlap
ball around the root of it. The cone measures six inches in length minus

the short stem; the stem extends into the axis around which whorl
forty-two wood-like scales. Under each scale a pair of seeds with blunt
single wings like aged paper once hid until the cone in its second
year flared open and released them into the paws of a ground squirrel.

Turn the pinecone to the left if you can hear me from the Connecticut
Turnpike of your afterlife. I'll stroke with focus my left thumb on
adjacent scales for hidden music. The longer I look at it the more human
the pinecone becomes as I become less one the longer I look at it.

The squirrel ate a portion of the seeds at once, tucked the remainder
in its cheeks to carry them back to its nest in the fieldstone wall
around the ruined flowerbed where foxglove used to grow. Meanwhile,
cells in your body had started going wrong. Not that I understand or

can pretend to. Turn the pinecone to the right if you hear me still.
Deep in the brain of invertebrates, the pineal gland gets its name from
its resemblance to a pinecone. Anatomists also call it the conarium
for the same reason. Melatonin factory, vestigial third eye, storied portal

to higher dimensions. The cone weighs approximately half an ounce, or
as many as five ruby-throated hummingbirds. How is it we think
next to nothing of what a hummingbird weighs, or what the bobolink
eats (rice, seeds, grains), or how it might feel to descend from dinosaur

to morsel. We exist in relation to the totality but choose to consider
the smallest portion of it possible. Demonstrate with the pinecone
what awareness outside the constraint of time feels like, if you can.
Foxglove prefer moist, rich, slightly acidic soil. I sliced my forefinger

with a knife on your Klonopin tonight cooking dinner for my family.
I did and didn't feel it. I think you knew I wouldn't have it in me to hurt
for long and when I did I died the way when made to feel like dirt
in the first place you come back partway dead or ready for it anyway.

All the while the cone of the white pine was the state flower of Maine.
It's the nonsense I miss. When people quarrel they forget for a time
that life is meaningless. Our last ended in me admitting to become
a parent solves nothing actually. The pinecone seems like it has a stain

from sap and rain. A wash. I wish the days I'm left were for planting
trees again instead of watering window-box impatiens and confinement.
Here in my hand a cone from the beautiful eastern white pine sits
stone still. Keep it that way. It isn't true that hummingbirds can't sing:

I hear them in my head all spring as a seed lost in the squirrel's haste
trembles into the pine whose cone I contain long after I set it down to rest.

Poem Written with an
Arrowhead in My Mouth

Again the sound of quartz pounding quartz
into Neolithic spear points
to be hafted onto shafts with tree-resin glue
and a twine made of fibers harvested from dead plants
comforts me as it keeps me
awake nights, leaving me feeling equally
provided for and covered in blood.

Again history's blistery tongue in my ear blurts
the cave of the belly goes
deeper than thought, and is less wholesome:
the vapors of the breath condense there, sour
by the hour on the walls, advancing
into pools whose surfaces strobe in archaic code
and whose depths cradle my kind of salamander.

At what point in the mud does an act of what
might be called independence become
possible is the question
on all of our limbs, not minds, not yet, although
we're getting there bit by bit, and then
we'll plateau for a period before gliding back
down into the huddle, dragging everything with us.

And when the future arrives in its vehicles
to poke through the mineralized
forms we leave behind, will we all be one to its eye,
or will it make a difference who
among us tried to stop ourselves, or tried to stop those
in charge, or whether any of us put their young
to sleep at the end, and if with poison, or with song?

Flamin' Hot Cheetos

When I sensed I might
belong, I drew

the cotton duck drape
that hung before

the patio door
to the residency's

clean white space
to seal me in, to seal

me in,
but my hand had been

where it had been,

and the stain it made
is blazon of my house.

The Lighthouse of Alexandria

Those figures in our literature who walk alone through cemeteries
    mouthing what they read on toppled headstones inwardly

are just trying to connect with people in a way they feel
    less threatened by. A number of us still don't find it natural

anymore to be among the living, not knowing what to speak,
    when to shut it down, or why to hold oneself oblique

to others mothers violence and a kind of gnarled-up sense
    of syntax I wouldn't wish on anyone. Even when its excellence

pushes back in one's defense. As in a backseat just last week
    I witnessed hatred amp up eyes I couldn't contradict provoke

in me some pride. I'll hate myself myself, not at someone else's
    instigation. And so it is we wade: on and into impulses

governing the many, dis-governing, trusting a counterforce
    from behind the desk of self-image and -interest will coerce

the animal in us back into its box-length tension. It doesn't
    always, and often you can smell it smolder under pleasant

workaday exchanges choking airspace even when it does.
But then, by the window: graffitied water towers, antennas'

metal toothpicks on rooftops: evidence of the absent. An elephant
caravan crosses Brooklyn Bridge as British and Hessian

troops kill Maryland soldiers (256) in front of my daughter's
school of brick and mortar. Up North, on a splashed white horse

and a bay, Wamsutta and Metacomet, sons of Wampanoag
sachem Massasoit, dead but a week, stop at a cranberry bog

on their way to Plymouth to adopt new names: Alexander
and Philip, hoping to feel a little of their father's friendlier

connection to the colonists. But with a decade of more life lost
to unchecked expansion, overhunting, shame, and a holocaust

of European diseases, King Philip will push back against the
arrogance after one last taste of it in late June with a lengthy

full-scale war that ends with his quartered body hanging like
garland in a tree, his head from a swamp in Bristol on a pike

carried up to Plymouth for political purposes, not too unlike those
motivating Ptolemy to hijack the long lavish funeral pro-

cession of Alexander the Great, digressing his body from a path
to Macedonia and into Egypt instead. He knew death

would make more of Alexander than life itself had, and whatever
city his tomb sat in would be a jewel to humanity forever.

That's what he wanted for Alexandria. City whose namesake
founder dreamed a vision of an isle in front of Egypt that broke

the progress of the stormy sea. He had read about it in Homer,
and here it was at last: Pharos, steadfast in the harbor

nature made and engineering divided in half with a bridge.
City of seabirds eating barley meant for cakes and porridge

but used to outline unbuilt buildings when they ran out of chalk.
City whose lighthouse served ends practical and symbolic

at once: bright limestone, 400 feet high, it made the flat port visible
to vessels at sea, even by day, and guided nearer vessels

through hazardous shoal waters. And more, it would stand for
the city's wealth, and its chutzpah, offering views of the splendor

of the ocean and the polis alike. It cast complex Alexander
in a fine posthumous light, and likewise acted as reminder

of Zeus's goodwill toward travelers by sea (a statue of him kept
watch from the roof). It brought the world to Egypt, Egypt

into the future. Ptolemy started the project and Ptolemy
II saw it to completion, which demonstrated the integrity

of the Ptolemaic dynasty, up to and including Cleopatra almost
    three centuries later. And by extension, it came to suggest

what we make connects the living to the dead, or it can if we take
    pains to secure it against tides, Romans, and one earthquake

after another. Conversely, it connects the dead to the living
    in a way they feel less threatened by, and then even the living

to life itself, which is a study of connections, as architecture is,
    such that if I fear myself, what I am fearing is all of us, but for us.

Roof

We hope for better things. A magnitude, a quantity
that can't be packed with ease like five into a quincunx
pattern on the die, or likewise echoed through the tree trunks'

placement in an orchard. Here the branches of an apple
fan like fingers from a hand, its forearm twisting up
through dirt to demonstrate revival, even to the doubter

who pokes at holy wounds to test their authenticity.
We want what we don't know, or what we know of mostly
through a long furnaceous rumbling lack of it composes

piecewise into numbers the choir of our never having
had it sings, not so much to give release as to give shape to
what we welcome back in finer form, in robes the color

of the Nile flowing north inside a child's encyclopedia.
When I felt the climbing up at first I meant to swallow it.
Tried to pen it in my lungs. Couldn't think of anyone

ever making sentences equal to the miracle I felt I was
containing. No rinse of recollection of any having heard.
Sank reasonable the urge to tamp that river in me down

on account of its immeasure. But we spare no length
for pleasure, know no room for reason when the crowd of us
amasses. These are our circumstances. To not know how

to demonstrate it doesn't mean doesn't exist, a cracked-
open pyramid amid the basic grasses of a life. We could be
contented with the cow of it, somehow, but we can't.

We hope for things better. An amplitude, some pressure
counter to the dominant. We build a roof above our head
to limn the need to raise it, an orange compliment paid

to the waves above Detroit, its blue light scattered bluer
by particles no citizen can put a pin in, by an ember against
a gray we stand under, knowing what rises from the ashes.

Burning Lichen from
a Bronze Age Megalith

Never before in the wind indigenous
   to the Atlantic have I felt
      commonsensical to myself, and now
         is no time
to start: loud power, constant
   boom, I have wanted to live
      like this in the longform, the way
         a plant can
         on air, suspended in
its element, swallowed whole
   by the senses: cold clear sky,
      companionable sun, no need
      not answered, all alien
to advanced thought, which has only
         ever brought more suffering.

Not technically a plant, not even one
   thing, but the mutually
      beneficial union of a fungus and green
      and/or blue-green
      algae, you've been with me
in the longform, long enough

for me to forget I didn't

   fold you up in the clear

      of a Ziploc, which is how it

looked, but in a hotel shower cap

   that, if I hadn't,

      would have one day clung to the head

      of a fellow traveler I'll never

   know, keeping hair dry, which is why

         it was put there, and I'm sorry.

Elsewhere, another traveler caught

   my attention once, saying

      you dropped something back there

      on the sidewalk

and automatically I thanked her

   without asking what

      it looked like I had dropped

      so I spent the next

         ten minutes looking for what

I didn't know, which is a rare

   and almost holy state of mind

      I couldn't wait to be

      released from—then there

you were, my little two-inch square

      of lichen fallen out of the open

pouch of my backpack. Now, brow

   riddled with the storms of

administration, I lay the green-gray
threads of you
on a block of dried-out peat
like a sugar cube and light it
in order to inhale
whatever principle of the sea
your filaments might
retain, or of the sea-blown
air you grew in, or of the rock
you anchored to before
I tore you off it, its purpose
uncertain, your smoke bitter, but enough
of an obstruction to see through.

Insomnia

As darkness dissolves
the forms of things

they appear to merge
into the one

unbroken substance
they have been

all along, no single
component of which

can be said to exist
by necessity, but with

such continuous
relation to all other

components, it's as if
nothing can be

lost without change
to everything, nothing

can be lost without
losing everything.

Hymn to Life

There were no American lions. No pygmy mammoths left
or giant short-faced bears, which towered over ten feet high
when rearing up on their haunches. There were no stout-
legged llamas, stilt-legged llamas, no single Yukon horse. The last
of the teratorns, its wingspan broader than the room in
which I'm writing now, had long since landed on a tar pit's

surface and was lost. There might be other things to think of
strobing in the fume or sometimes poking through the thick of it
like the tiny golden toads once so prevalent in the cloud
forests north of Monteverde, only none of them are living
anywhere anymore. The last was seen on May 15, 1989, the week
Bon Jovi's "I'll Be There for You" topped Billboard's Hot 100.

Then it dropped to three. A teratorn might have fit in here
the long way come to think of it. Studies claim it wasn't
climate change that killed the golden toad but a fungal epidemic
provoked by cyclical weather patterns. Little things like that
had a way of disappearing: thimbles, the Rocky Mountain
grasshopper, half the hearing in my patient ear. There were

no eastern elk, no sea mink, and no heath hens, a distinct
subspecies of the prairie chicken. Once common to the coastland
barrens of New Hampshire down to Virginia, they're often thought
to have been eaten in favor of wild turkey at the inaugural
Thanksgiving feast. To work on my character I pretend to be
traveling Portsmouth to Arlington in modern garb at first,

then backwards into costumes of the past: T-shirt and shorts,
gray flannel suit, a cutaway jacket and matching breeches
tucked into boots, taupe velvet getup with ruffles and ribbons
streaming into Delaware till I'm buckled like a Puritan, musket
in hand, not half-famished, and there's plenty of heath hens
everywhere I look. But there were still no Carolina parakeets

and no Smith Island cottontails, a long-contested subspecies
of the eastern cottontail. These lost rabbits, somewhat shaggier
than their mainland cousins, were named for the barrier
island off the tip of Virginia's Eastern Shore, where Thomas Dale,
deputy governor of the Virginia Colony, set up a saltworks
back in 1614, and not for the Chesapeake's other Smith Island

up in Maryland, birthplace of the Smith Island cake, that state's
only official dessert—a venerable confection whose pencil-
thin layers, numbering eight to twelve on average, lie divided
by a fudge-like frosting cooked for greater lastingness, making it
suitable for local oystermen to take with them on the long
autumn harvest. Smith Island in Washington offers nesting

sites for tufted puffins on its rocky cliff faces as well as rest
stations for migrant sea lions. Situated in Long Island Sound,
Connecticut's Smith Island is among that state's famed Thimble
Islands, a cluster of landmasses named for the thimbleberry,
cousin to the black raspberry. During the Revolutionary War,
the Thimbles were deforested to rid the sound of hiding

places for British ships. Alabama boasts no fewer than three
Smith Islands. Little can be said about the one in Minnesota's
Voyageurs National Park. Its neighboring islands include
Rabbit, Snake, Wolf, Wigwam, Sweetnose, and Twin Alligator
down here on the American side, and Little Dry, Big, and Big Dry
up on the Canadian. Tomorrow should be 82° and sunny

but it won't be. The blue pike cavorted through the waters
of the Great Lakes no longer. Ditto the somber blackfin cisco.
Overfishing, pollution, and the introduction of nonnative
species did both fish in as early as 1960 and '70, respectively.
There were no spectacled cormorants, no Goff's pocket gophers,
and no Ainsworth's salamanders, a species known to us only

through two specimens found on Ainsworth family property
in Mississippi on June 12, 1964. That same day Nelson Mandela
was sentenced to life in prison. I remember the feeling of
another kind, the way they alternately lay limp in my hands
then pleaded to be free. They took naps in the dampness
of softened logs. There's a fine dirt, a dust I guess, that collects

under the rug I'm sitting on. I think the rough weave of it
acts as rasp to our foot-bottoms then sieve to what it loosens.
There were no Caribbean monk seals, eight of which no less
than Christopher Columbus killed for food in 1494, and therefore
no Caribbean monk seal nasal mites, an objectively hideous
arachnoid parasite that resided nowhere but in the respiratory

passages of the *Monachus tropicalis.* When it occurs to me I
sweep it up. Back in the day they used to darken our skies
in flocks a mile wide and 300 miles in length, enough to feather
the air from Fall River down to Philadelphia, their peak
population hovering above five billion, or 40% of the total
roll of birds in North America, but there were no remaining

passenger pigeons, the last of their red eyes having shut
in Cincinnati on September 1, 1914. Her name was Martha.
Martha Washington went by Patsy as a child. Her pet raccoon
was Nosey. Cozumel Island's pygmy raccoon is actually a distinct
species and not, like the Barbados raccoon, a subspecies
of the common. There might be as few as 250 of the former

hidden in the mangroves or prowling the wetlands for ghost
crabs and lizards, whereas the latter was last seen in '64
when one was struck dead by a car in Bathsheba, a fishing village
built on Barbados's eastern shore, magnet for hurricanes
and pro surfers, its foamy white waters calling to mind
the milk baths rumored to have kept Solomon's mother so

perilously beautiful. First the milk's lactic acid would have
acted as an exfoliant, gently removing layers of the dead,
dry skin to uncover younger, fresher skin waiting like artwork
in Dunkirk underneath, then the milk's natural fat content
would restore moisture lost to the exacting atmosphere
of biblical Jerusalem, whose name in Hebrew, *yireh shalem,*

means "will see peace." Most versions of the story make her
into an exhibitionist but the Midrash says Bathsheba, modest,
was washing behind a wicker screen when Satan, seizing
opportunity, appeared as a red bird to David who, cocksure
with projectiles now, aimed the stone in his hands at the bird
but hit the screen instead, splitting it in half and thereby

revealing our bather, the wife of Uriah the Hittite at the time
but not for much longer. All these gains and losses, so mysterious
from a distance, held together it has felt by nothing stronger
than momentum, like a series of bicycle accidents or a pattern
in the pomegranate, come to hint at a logic in time, but whether
it's more fitting to say that they promise to reveal it or else

threaten to is debatable. Attempts to stem the vast mosquito
population in salt marshes abutting Kennedy Space Center
on Florida's Merritt Island, technically a peninsula but more like
a question mark of land flopped into the Atlantic, devastated
the dusky seaside sparrow. Its last known specimen died
on June 17, 1987, when the ballad "Always" by Atlantic Starr

dominated radio. Mosquitoes would have taken to the nasty
Olduvai waterhole around which two clans of hominids battle
at the start of Stanley Kubrick's *2001: A Space Odyssey.* This is after
the first monolith shows up. The film's monoliths are artifacts
of alien origin, identical in ratio but varying in size, designed
to provoke large-scale changes in human life. As when it dawns

on the wiry leader of the clan the first monolith appears to
to bludgeon the other to death with a leg bone. Later on he hurls it
into the air to celebrate his power, the image of its tumbling
weaponhood at half-speed match-cutting to that of a long
white nuclear satellite angled in orbit against the scintillant
anthracite of space. Pan right to Earth, or a quarter of it silvery

blue in the corner, aloofly beautiful for sure but only a pale
idea of a planet when set beside photographs taken years later
by the crew of Apollo 17 on December 7, 1972, *annus finalis*
for the Lake Pedder earthworm, bush wren, and possibly
the Toolache wallaby as well, long considered among kangaroos
to have been the most elegant. The sapphire blue, the ochre

of Africa, the chalk-white spirals convolving as if an icecap's
wispy tentacles. They were killed for fur, sport, and frequently
with the aid of greyhounds, who hunt mostly by way of sight
as opposed to scent. Then Earth is at the left as the satellite
approaches it almost dozily to the opening bars of Strauss's
"Blue Danube," first performed on February 15, 1867, in the now-

defunct Diana Ballroom. In my own Diana Ballroom, named
not for the Roman goddess of the hunt, the moon, and chastity
directly, but by way of the two-kilometer lunar crater christened
in her honor in 1979, declivity in whose embrace my ballroom
trembles comfortably, I boost my chi by remembering to breathe
deep, to eat oatmeal, ginger, and figs, and to commit myself

to a custody of wildflowers, up to and including the maroon
perfume of the chocolate cosmos, a non-self-pollinating species
whose every plant now in bloom is a clone of the selfsame
specimen uprooted from a cubic foot of Mexico back in 1902.
Likewise the last known Rocky Mountain locust ever to appear
appeared alone that year on a prairie up in Canada, whereas

decades before a glistering storm of them blanketed an area
vast as California, matter-of-factly devouring buckwheat, barley,
strawberries, apple trees, fence posts, and even the laundry
wildly flapping away on the line, the sound of "millions of jaws
biting and chewing" setting a nation's nerves on edge, or at least
Laura Ingalls Wilder's, if we're to believe her *On the Banks*

of Plum Creek, first of three books spectered by prototypical
beeotch Nellie Oleson. Cloudiness persists regarding the difference
between locust and grasshopper. Typically I keep a number
of soaps on hand and seem to know by instinct which of them
to reach for. In gingham and curls Nellie Oleson was played
by Alison Arngrim in the 1970s TV adaptation. The Wife of Bath

was also an Alison. An Angrim is father to the outlaw Gorlim
in Tolkien's Middle-Earth mythos. They say to run the tap
as hot as you can stand. Fast forward a century to April 16, 2002,
and dance anthem "Hot in Herre" by Cornell Haynes Jr., better
known to us as Nelly, reaches number one and reigns there
seven weeks. Miss Oleson, elder offspring of the local retailer,

is based on no fewer than three distinct historical persons.
Produced by The Neptunes, "Hot in Herre" samples Neil Young's
track "There's a World" and lifts its hook from an infinitely
more upbeat "Bustin' Loose" by Chuck Brown. Later on or earlier
in 2002, up a slope in dewy Mauna Loa, a Nelly somewhere
on the radio, the last pair of noncaptive Hawaiian crows flew

into the category known as "extinct in the wild." "We are leaving,
we are gone," Young sings wanly atop percussion and strings
courtesy of the London Symphony Orchestra. "Come with us
to all alone." 'Alala is the word for the Hawaiian crow in Hawaiian.
No fewer than twenty 'alala chicks were hatched in 2012 in
a breeding facility at San Diego Zoo. Jack Nitzsche co-produced

and also played piano. "Bustin' loose to my love Jones," declares
the late great Brown, dead in Baltimore mid-May of that year.
"Bustin' loose to each his own." He traded cigarettes for a guitar
while serving time in Virginia's historic Lorton Reformatory.
An average daytime temperature of 89°. He was father to the style
of music known as go-go, so-called because the sound, Brown

was said to have said, "just goes and goes." But there were no
dire wolves, no Florida black wolves, and no Texas reds,
although the red, morphologically midway between the gray
and the coyote, has been bred in captivity down on South Carolina's
Bull's Island since 1987, year Tim Tebow was born and Andy
Warhol died. Likewise the year in which the films *Precious, Fargo,*

and *American Psycho* are set. "It can be hard to tell," the *Times*
admits of the thousands who once posed for photographs in
the posture known as "tebowing," whether they intended to celebrate
or to mock the quarterback for his much-publicized virtuous ways.
Nor were there any of the subspecies indigenous to Canada's
Banks Island, Earth's twenty-fourth largest island, upon which

the first confirmed wild hybrid of the polar bear and grizzly
was found and shot in 2006. The island also has the distinction
of its treelessness, and of being home to fleets of musk oxen.
Times I count myself among them if more comfortable in my bulk
I still can't get around the funk of us. Our ancient mouths
set to decimating herbages. In times of risk we assume the O-

shaped formation around our wobbly young. A sense of calm
or guiltlessness blows in. Then it's back to business with another
cup of coffee, hot beverage held to have been first drunk in
these parts in 1668, when frothy infusions of the slow-roasted bean
spiked with costly cinnamon sticks and honey grew popular
along New Amsterdam's foggy docks. In tidepools to the north

eelgrass limpets affixed to eelgrass blithely at the time, unaware
an insidious slime mold campaign would in centuries inflict
catastrophe on their habitat, making them the first marine
invertebrate to dissolve in the historical era, the last of its kind
plucked while the Bank of Manhattan Trust Building whistled up
past the Woolworth like a startled monk's apocalyptic vision

of a cloud-bound train. It began in 1929. Sir Hubert Wilkins,
Arctic explorer, advocated in *The Advertiser* for submarine
technology as tomorrow's answer to the Northwest Passage's
pack-ice question. Ice had heretofore kept a surface-travel route
troublingly out of reach, even after its putative discovery
by Sir Robert McClure, who on his eastward voyage spotted

from atop a windy Banks Island promontory the westmost
landmass mapped three decades earlier by Sir William Parry.
McClure later lent his name, understood to translate to "son of a
sallow lad," to a lunar crater whose diameter spans over
twelve times that of Diana, but only a quarter that of the big
kahuna Tycho, where a second monolith appears. This one emits

a painful radio signal to a third, which orbits like an onyx
football field around Jupiter. Rewind 150 years and McClure's
HMS *Investigator*, like a *Musca domestica* on a runway paved
with flypaper, has come to a full stop in the blind white grip of ice.
It felt like 1850. There were no Steller's sea cows, the tame
kelp-nibbling cousins to the manatee, albeit double their size,

and there were no great auks. The last known pair of them
was claimed on July 3, 1844, by poachers hired by a merchant
itching for tchotchkes to ornament an office. Nine long
winters later, rescue sledges bundled McClure and crew up
and sped them back to the claps of Britain. Soon Banks Island's
musk ox population whittled down to nil as their flesh gave

way to the hungry Inuit who trekked up to 300 miles to strip
McClure's abandoned ship before the ice crushed her completely,
folding her metals into Mercy Bay. "I took him by the neck
and he flapped his wings," the poacher said. "He made no cry."
Inuit shaped *Investigator*'s copper and iron into spear- and arrow-
heads as well as knife blades, chisels, and harpoons like those

depicted in lithographs in the mitts of seal hunters patiently
stationed at breathing holes in the ice. But there were no
broad-leaved centaury plants, no western sassafras, and no
Galápagos amaranth, cousin to the seabreach amaranth. Its tiny
spinach-like leaves once bounced along dunes from South
Carolina to Massachusetts till habitat loss, insensitive beach-

grooming tactics, and recreational vehicles slashed figures
drastically. When ice decides it must feel like being splintered
from a multiplex of tightness that pains but holds together.
Aerial shot of 1961, year submarine thriller *K-19* and *Saving
Mr. Banks* are set in. Kennedy is president. The cloud of a hundred
musk oxen migrating back to Banks Island rises plainly as

narrow-leafed campion, a handful of whose seeds had slept
30 millennia before being found in 2007 in a ruined system
of ground squirrel burrows. Surveys will report up to 800
heads in 1967 and a thousand more in 1970. All matter thunder-
cracking belowdecks: hoof of earth into water, water over
air, air under water and up. So that the vessel, broken, settles

onto sea stars on the floor. The seeds were sown successfully
under grow lights in Siberia, deep in whose permafrost
international high-fiving scientists discovered a fully intact
woolly mammoth carcass. To enlarge my sympathy I attempt
to picture the loud tarp tents around the digging site, the lamp-
lengths they putter away to, the costs. By 1994, estimates

on the island ran as high as 84,000, over half the musk oxen
alive at the time, but paging ahead five years we see numbers
speedily hunted back down to 58,000, or as many pounds
of "fine ground beef" called back by California's Central Valley
Meat Company in 2013 when "tiny pieces of plastic" were found
nestling in it like the voice of Katy Perry, whose hit "Roar"

was everywhere repeating we would hear it. "Called back"
says Emily Dickinson's epitaph. One scientist says to the other,
"What's that?" The other says, "Do you feel it, Slovo? A certain
category of effect. Difficult to describe and yet a certain category
of effect is still possible. You'd think it would have wizened
in our atmosphere by now, or withdrawn in sickness or mere

tedium into the cold shell of itself in the manner of a what,

yes, a gastropod, the very figure of a recluse, secular of course,

anthropomorphic misnomer because its foot is not actually

its stomach, witness the oblong rocksnail, still another thought

extinct due to rampant habitat loss but no, not yet, Alabama

graduate student Nathan Whelan just now located a specimen

kayaking down the Cahaba River, misplaced modifier Slovo

it is the student in the kayak, not the snail, *badum tish*, but

amid the mist and as if against this vanishment of dodos a certain

category persists, not unlike a last known pair of Middlemist's

Red camellia, a cultivar sent as rootstock to England from

China by John Middlemist in 1804." Note: One is in a garden

in New Zealand, where the laughing owl is no longer, thanks

largely to cats. Its call has been described as "a loud cry

made up of a series of dismal shrieks frequently repeated,"

"a peculiar barking noise . . . just like the barking of a young dog,"

"precisely the same as two men 'cooeying' to each other

from a distance," and "a melancholy hooting note," to quote

The Owl Pages, sweet dream of a website whose first FAQ asks,

"I've seen an owl, can you tell me what kind it is?" The other

Middlemist's Red, long presumed barren, resides in a nursery

somewhere in Britain, and stalwart through its hardships,

it has begun to bloom again. The remains of the *Investigator*

found in 2010 were well preserved by the pristine cold waters

of the Canadian Arctic. And yet no one's idea of red includes
the hue of Middlemist's camellia, which is instead a true
pink, or some might even say a rose. Mallarmé would just say
"flower" and from oblivion there would arise musically a flower
absent from all bouquets. "Whoever reaches into a rosebush,"
Lou Andreas-Salomé supposed, "may seize a handful of flowers;

but no matter how many one holds, it's only a small portion
of the whole. Nevertheless, a handful is enough to experience
the nature of the flowers. Only if we refuse to reach into the bush,
because we can't possibly seize all the flowers at once, or if
we spread out our handful of roses as if it were the *whole*
bush itself—only then does it bloom apart from us, unknown

to us, and we are left alone." Endangered coastal roses seek
some subtler way of putting it. "All the roses in the world," Rilke
gushed to Salomé—whose Galilean namesake, it's often over-
looked, didn't desire the head of John the Baptist for herself but
was told to ask for it by her mother, Herodias, whose union
with Herod Antipas, at once her uncle and her brother-in-law,

John declared unlawful—"bloom for you and through you."
Forget-me-nots bloom unhindered in Heidelberg, where Max Wolf
spied in 1905 a so-called minor planet he named 526 Salome.
That these odd bodies spatter the galaxy like pollen shaken
from a central flower, or like honeybees tumbling along with us
around the sun, I never knew until a visit to the Minor Planet

Center website at a turning point like April 1543. I think I saw
upwards of 3,500 were spotted last month alone. "Nature is
an inexplicable problem," Emily Brontë wrote in 1842 in French
in a confection titled "The Butterfly." "It exists on a principle
of destruction." Lepidopterists are scouring Florida's pine forests
and gentle coastal jungles on the trail of five butterfly species

feared as good as gone. They were never listed as endangered
and still aren't known to be extinct. These are their names:
Zestos skipper. Rockland Meske's skipper. Zarucco duskywing.
Bahamian swallowtail. Nickerbean blue. "I love you," wrote Salomé,
"with all your harms," who died in her sleep shortly after
the Gestapo destroyed her library, in her poem "Hymn to Life."

Her friend Nietzsche liked the poem so much he set it to music.
I've listened to it and can't say I like it but I'm listening to it
again as I try to finish. I promised Lynn I'd put the dishes away
before the babysitter arrives but it looks like I won't be a person
of my word tonight. I had meant to write about the imperial
woodpecker of Mexico. The red gazelle. I told my friend Dottie

when saddened in the predawn I have seen the people pushing
small mountains of soda cans in their shopping carts stop
in front of my recycling, open one bag after another of empty
metal and glass, dig through them, take what they need and shut
the bags back up with so much care it has destroyed me. I remember
bathing my daughter when she was two and how I stopped

short thinking if I were gone tomorrow she wouldn't even
remember. The year was 2007. Radio waves associated with
cellphones may not have been contributing to recent declines in
bee population. "And if you must destroy me," says the poem,
"I'll tear myself away from you / As I would leave a friend."
When there was time to put away the dishes, they were gone.

E HUMAN NOTES AND ACKNOWLEDGMENTS AND THE HUMAN NOTES AND ACK
GMENTS AND THE HUMAN NOTES AND ACKNOWLEDGMENTS AND THE HUMAN
D ACKNOWLEDGMENTS AND THE HUMAN NOTES AND ACKNOWLEDGMENTS AN
MAN NOTES AND ACKNOWLEDGMENTS AND THE HUMAN NOTES AND ACKNOW
NTS AND THE HUMAN NOTES AND ACKNOWLEDGMENTS AND THE HUMAN NOT
KNOWLEDGMENTS AND THE HUMAN NOTES AND ACKNOWLEDGMENTS AND TH
MAN NOTES AND ACKNOWLEDGMENTS AND THE HUMAN NOTES AND ACKNOW
NTS AND THE HUMAN NOTES AND ACKNOWLEDGMENTS AND THE HUMAN NOT
KNOWLEDGMENTS AND THE HUMAN NOTES AND ACKNOWLEDGMENTS AND TH
MAN NOTES AND ACKNOWLEDGMENTS AND THE HUMAN NOTES AND ACKNOW
NTS AND THE HUMAN NOTES AND ACKNOWLEDGMENTS AND THE HUMAN NOT
KNOWLEDGMENTS AND THE HUMAN NOTES AND ACKNOWLEDGMENTS AND TH
MAN NOTES AND ACKNOWLEDGMENTS AND THE HUMAN NOTES AND ACKNOW
NTS AND THE HUMAN NOTES AND ACKNOWLEDGMENTS AND THE HUMAN NOT
KNOWLEDGMENTS AND THE HUMAN NOTES AND ACKNOWLEDGMENTS AND TH
MAN NOTES AND ACKNOWLEDGMENTS AND THE HUMAN NOTES AND ACKNOW
NTS AND THE HUMAN NOTES AND ACKNOWLEDGMENTS AND THE HUMAN NOT
KNOWLEDGMENTS AND THE HUMAN NOTES AND ACKNOWLEDGMENTS AND TH
MAN NOTES AND ACKNOWLEDGMENTS AND THE HUMAN NOTES AND ACKNOW
NTS AND THE HUMAN NOTES AND ACKNOWLEDGMENTS AND THE HUMAN NOT
KNOWLEDGMENTS AND THE HUMAN NOTES AND ACKNOWLEDGMENTS AND TH
MAN NOTES AND ACKNOWLEDGMENTS AND THE HUMAN NOTES AND ACKNOW
NTS AND THE HUMAN NOTES AND ACKNOWLEDGMENTS AND THE HUMAN NOT
KNOWLEDGMENTS AND THE HUMAN NOTES AND ACKNOWLEDGMENTS AND TH
MAN NOTES AND ACKNOWLEDGMENTS AND THE HUMAN NOTES AND ACKNOW
NTS AND THE HUMAN NOTES AND ACKNOWLEDGMENTS AND THE HUMAN NOT
KNOWLEDGMENTS AND THE HUMAN NOTES AND ACKNOWLEDGMENTS AND TH
MAN NOTES AND ACKNOWLEDGMENTS AND THE HUMAN NOTES AND ACKNOW
NTS AND THE HUMAN NOTES AND ACKNOWLEDGMENTS AND THE HUMAN NOT
KNOWLEDGMENTS AND THE HUMAN NOTES AND ACKNOWLEDGMENTS AND TH
MAN NOTES AND ACKNOWLEDGMENTS AND THE HUMAN NOTES AND ACKNOW
NTS AND THE HUMAN NOTES AND ACKNOWLEDGMENTS AND THE HUMAN NOT

Notes

The epigraph is from Alfred Tennyson's *In Memoriam.*

What Is Real takes its title from a book by Giorgio Agamben (translated by Lorenzo Chiesa) and another by Adam Becker. The poem adapts a passage from Virginia Woolf's *To the Lighthouse* and an idea from Jean Baudrillard's *America* (translated by Chris Turner).

The Stars Down to Earth takes its title from an essay by Theodor Adorno. This poem is for Brett Fletcher Lauer.

The Endless is for Max Ritvo.

The Problem of the Many takes its title from, and refracts some ideas in, an essay by Peter Unger.

Arrows from the Sun adapts its title from the song "Myth" by Beach House, whose music held my hand the whole time.

By Night with Torch and Spear takes its title from a short film by Joseph Cornell.

A Habitation of Jackals, a Court for Ostriches takes its title from Isaiah 34:13.

The Radiance of a Thousand Suns takes its title from the Bhagavad Gita as quoted by J. Robert Oppenheimer. This poem is for Stella Donnelly.

All the Shrimp I Can Eat is dedicated to Richard Howard. I thought he said life might be nothing more than a trip through the digestive tract of a deity, but that isn't what he said at all.

Lunch in a Town Named After a Company Slowly Poisoning Its Residents is for Ricardo Maldonado.

After Callimachus takes its initial inspiration from "Against the Telchines," the name commonly given to the prologue to Callimachus's *Aetia.*

Escape into Time takes its title from an engraving by Peter J. Grippe.

Traveler is for Ada Donnelly.

The Death of the Author takes its title from an essay by Roland Barthes. This poem is dedicated to Scott and Kathy Pitcock and to the Benny's on Putnam Pike in Greenville, RI (now closed).

The Death of Truth takes its title from a book by Michiko Kakutani.

NyQuil is for, and after, Mark Strand.

Leviathan adapts some of its lexicon from the discussion of Hobbes's *Leviathan* in Jonathan Crary's book *24/7.*

Mutual Life is adapted from Shakespeare's "Sonnet 100."

Levitation adapts a sentence from *The Life of Saint Teresa of Avila by Herself* (translated by J. M. Cohen) and another from *Flying Saucers Have Landed* by Desmond Leslie and George Adamski.

Some Comforts at the Expense of Others adapts its title from a phrase in Jonathan Crary's *24/7.*

Poem Interrupted by Whitesnake incorporates a passage from Whitesnake's "Here I Go Again," written by David Coverdale and Bernie Marsden. This poem is for Whitesnake and for the Met Foods supermarket on Henry Street in Brooklyn (now closed).

Insomnia is indebted, in part, to Emmanuel Levinas's discussion of insomnia in *Existence and Existents* (translated by Alphonso Lingis).

Hymn to Life is dedicated to David Skeist, James Rutherford, Laura Butler Rivera, and everyone in their ensemble, who have been adapting it into a multidisciplinary performance piece since 2015. Their artistry and commitment have given me hope.

Acknowledgments

I am grateful to all the family, friends, and colleagues who encouraged me throughout the writing of this book, especially Mary Jo Bang, Alan Gilbert, Jeff Hipsher, Dorothea Lasky, Brett Fletcher Lauer, and Elizabeth Metzger, who were first to lay eyes on many of these poems. In particular, I am grateful to Eleanor Sarasohn, whose editorial genius and dedication to this book in manuscript form had enormous impact on its final state. I don't know where, much less how, to begin thanking Lynn Melnick, who suffered every twist and turn and all the sleep deficits that transpired during the writing of this book, who weathered all the setbacks and celebrated the achievements, who shared in all the tragedies and made the miracles possible. I will always love you. I am grateful, too, to my parents and to my daughters, and I will never be done thanking Peter Sacks and Lucie Brock-Broido for their life-saving mentorships. I am thankful, too, to so many others, living and dead—too many to name here individually—who offered me moral and practical support at some point during, if not throughout, the eight years in which this book was written.

Grateful acknowledgment is made to the John Simon Guggenheim Memorial Foundation for awarding me a fellowship to support the writing of this book, and likewise to the Lannan Foundation and to the T. S. Eliot Foundation for providing me with generous residencies during which many of these poems were completed. Thanks are due, too, to Columbia University for its investment in my work and for providing me with stable employment and a brilliant community of artists. I am also thankful to Erin Belieu for choosing a selection of these poems for the Poetry Society of America's Alice Fay di Castagnola Award for a manuscript in progress. No end of thanks to Matthew Zapruder for his faith and guidance, and to Charlie, Heidi, Blyss, Ryo, and everyone at Wave Books for helping to pull this book together.

Grateful acknowledgment is also made to the editors of the following periodicals and websites where these poems originally appeared: *American Poetry Review*: Levitation; Poem Written with a Pinecone in My Hand; *A Public Space*: Apologies from the Ground Up; The Stars Down to Earth; *Art in Print*: Escape into Time; *The Baffler*: Chemical Life; *The Believer*: Golden; *BOMB*: Burning Lichen from a Bronze Age Megalith; Happiness; Some Comforts at the Expense of Others; *The Cortland Review*: Fascination; *Hampden-Sydney Poetry Review*: Smartwater; *Harvard Review*: Traveler; *jubilat*: Gifted; *Lana Turner*: The Problem of the Many; *LA Review of Books Quarterly Journal*: The Death of the Author; The Death of Print Culture; *The Nation*: Solvitur Ambulando; *New England Review*: All Through the War; Poem Written with an Arrowhead in My Mouth; *The New Republic*: Poem on a Stair; the *New Yorker*: Diet Mountain Dew; Leviathan; Malamute; Unlimited Soup and Salad; *92y.org*: Lunch in a Town Named After a Company Slowly Poisoning Its Residents; *Oversound*: Arrows from the Sun; Insomnia; Lapis Lazuli; *The Paris Review*: After Callimachus; *Parnassus*: The Lighthouse of Alexandria; *Plume*: All the Shrimp I Can Eat; A Habitation of Jackals, a Court for Ostriches; *Poetry*: Hymn to Edmond Albius; Hymn to Life; *Poetry London*: Apologies from the Ground Up; Cursum Perficio; The Death of Truth; *Poetry Northwest*: The Earth Itself; *Poets.org*: By Night with Torch and Spear; The Endless; Lycopodium Obscurum; Poem Interrupted by Whitesnake; *Prelude*: Prometheus; *The Scores*: November Paraphrase; Stunt; *The Spectacle:* Flamin' Hot Cheetos; *Surface*: Roof; *T: The New York Times Style Magazine*: Shame; *Tupelo Quarterly*: What Is Real.

Grateful acknowledgement is also made to Sharmila Cohen and Paul Legault for publishing "Mutual Life" in *The Sonnets: Translating and Rewrit-*

ing Shakespeare, to Will Harris and Richard Osmund for publishing "Ny-Quil" in *The Mimic Octopus*, and to Daniel Lawless for publishing "The Radiance of a Thousand Suns" in *Plume Anthology of Poetry 7*. Thanks, too, to Denise Duhamel and David Lehman for including "Apologies from the Ground Up" in *The Best American Poetry 2013* and to Bill Henderson, Patricia Smith, and Arthur Sze for including "The Earth Itself" in the *Pushcart Prize XXXVIII: Best of the Small Presses 2014*, as well as to Jason Koo and Joe Pan for including it in *Brooklyn Poets Anthology*. And, lastly, I thank Dara Wier, Pam Glaven, Emily Pettit, Guy Pettit, and everyone at Factory Hollow Press for reprinting "Hymn to Life" in a beautiful limited edition chapbook.

The Human

In the interim I will find a way to feel at home with the animal
Aristotle in his *Politics* says nature made for politics

because alone among animals it enjoys the gift of speech.
Other animals have a voice to indicate what is pleasant,

what painful, and to relay it to each other, but true speech,
says Aristotle, takes things further, and is intended to make clear

what is beneficial, what harmful, what is good or bad,
and this among animals is peculiar to the human, who alone

enjoys perception of the just, which nature would never
provide without cause, he says, but does so that they might live

collectively, in communities, and not like those of the goat,
which seeks only what gives pleasure, and wanders

endlessly to avoid pain, but in settlements, vast cities
it takes politics to build, an effort extended across centuries

like bridges over waterways, their lengths reflected in the
flowing underneath them and up glass faces of towers the sun

illuminates with such intensity it feels like intention—
the will of what is to go on, to take things further, to adapt

parts of the body intended for breathing into a means to
force air into sounds, sounds into words, words into prayers of

thanks to the sun. And when I close my eyes to brace against
the late imperial effects of it, I feel a forebear step forward

from a cave in thought, its arms extended as if to take part
bodily in the beauty of what we call sky, and through some new

distortion in the throat, indicates what the many, still situated
in dark behind us, come one by one to tremble at the mouth to see.